Body Mind Soul Money

D.N. Howard and Associates

Copyright 2007 D.N. Howard and Associates

Published and Distributed in the United States by:

Howard-Hirsch Publishing
Green Ohio 44232

Book Design: Dawnetta Slaughter

All rights reserved.

Copyright Notice:

All materials contained in this book are protected by United States copyright law and may not be reproduced, distributed, transmitted, displayed, published or broadcast without the prior written permission of Howard Hirsch Publishing, the owner of the content. You may not alter or remove any trademark, copyright or other notice from content.

The author of this book does not dispense medical advice or prescribe the use of any technique as a form of treatment for medical or physical problems without the advice of a physician either directly or indirectly. The intent of the author is to offer information of a general nature to help you in your effort toward emotional, physical, spiritual and financial well-being. In the event you use any of the information contained in this book, which is your right, the author, publisher, and associates assume no responsibility for your actions or consequences resulting from those actions.

ISBN 10   0-9802307-7-2

ISBN 13   978 0-9802307-7-2

First Printing November 2007
Second Printing January 2008
Third Printing May 2018
Ebook 2018

Printed in USA

Other new books by

Howard-Hirsch Publishing

The Mend by T.Linsay Cole

Death Movements:
The Suicide Cult Phenomenon by T. Linsay Cole

Songs for the Sensual Soul
By Cyra Nightwine

For Children:
Ooble Booble

One Training Season

What if I told you that in ninety days you could feel like a completely different person?

What if I said that you could be more popular, not just because you could be **beautiful** on the outside, but because you could be **smarter, wittier, and more confident** on the inside?

What if I told you that you could have more **money**, **energy** and more **friends** in just ninety days?

Would you commit to *reading and following one page a day* in this book?

What if that's all it takes?

<u>**One page a day**</u> can change your life if you read and follow it for one 90-day "training season".

Will you give one training season to **change your life forever**?

You can:

- Teach your mind to accept knowledge easier and retrieve information faster.
- Strengthen your body and make it sleeker, smoother, and healthier.
- Strengthen your faith in your higher power or your inner conscience, with kindness and love.
- Put more money in your bank account and learn to put even pocket change to work for you.

You will find a new way of eating in this book. It's easier than you think and it works quickly.

You will find a new way of thinking on each page.
Start on page one, keep a journal of your transformation either in a notebook or on your phone or computer. (Look for our progress app coming soon or use MyFitnessPal.)

Everything in this book is easy, and even if you make minimal effort you can see big results in ninety days.

After 90 days, please connect with us online and let us know how your life has changed at BodyMindSoulMoney.com.

We thank you for giving us a few weeks of your time and wish you a wonderful life ahead.

A letter from D.N. Howard

Dear Reader,

Thank you for this minute of your valuable time. I want to welcome you to our latest attempt to make a positive change in the world.

This book is only one of many tools you can use to transform into who you've always wanted to be.

You are unique and exceptional. You live and learn in your own way. We understand that. This book is designed with that in mind Suggestions are given for tactile, visual, auditory and academic learning styles. Repetition of exercises helps make them habit.

We want to make it clear that it's a book of guidelines, not a military-precision manual. You will build your menu to better suit your tastes, but please stay within the plant-based, no-soy parameters for great results.

Also, don't underestimate the power of water. Plain ice water is tasteless but shaken with lemon/mint/ginger/maple syrup, it's delicious. **ICE COLD water is perhaps the most important part of the plan**, it can help you <u>passively burn up to 500 calories a day</u>.

Flavoring is important as well. Beans are boring but add salsa, or sautéed onions, peppers and a few herbs? Mmm. Eating protein regularly helps you retain muscle. <u>Muscle burns fat</u>. You need it protein!

If you really want to change, begin on page one, and do one page a day for ninety days. You CAN do it.

On behalf of myself and my staff, thank you and good luck.
Godspeed,
D.N. Howard

W.I.S.D.O.M. for Weight Loss

Walk at least half a mile a day.
(Use a chair? **W**heel half a mile!)

Isometrically tense and release lower abdominal, upper leg and upper arm muscles once an hour.
Hold for 60 seconds, release.

Shower in tepid or cool water to boost metabolism.
(Imagine the cool shower at the beach.)

Drink ice water, not sodium filled soda.
You are now salt-free.

Open your lungs and breathe deeply.
Expanding your oxygen intake gives you energy and burns calories passively!

Move throughout the day.
Gently stretch vital muscles whenever you can.

(**WISDOM** will help you lose weight and trim down **with no workouts** if you do it every day!)

The Food:

First: Start every meal with a glass of **ice water**.
For faster results, you can have a cup of tea a half an hour after eating, to bump up your energy and metabolism.
Instead of sugar, use **real** maple syrup.

Second: You will be stretching and contracting, not running or lifting. Get the weight off first, then sculpt yourself.

Finally, and most importantly: Eat until you want to stop. Yes, just eat. You will notice there is no limit on any of the food. That's because without dairy, meat, flour, sugar, salt, or oil, you'll eat a normal amount and get full faster.

You are now eating the way people ate before big corporations turned happy animals into products, imprisoning, mistreating, and injecting them with hormones. (This is important for your soul.)

You are now eating real food, not stuff in boxes that is processed with waste we used to throw away. *You are eating food you could grow yourself.*

You might be thinking, "We had a shorter life span then.". We also had no vaccines, little medicine, less food, and we didn't know about the importance of cleanliness.

This food *will* help you live longer. The fat you are carrying is killing you.

You can eat the consequence-free foods all day long and still lose weight. I call them "C-free foods" and I always have a bowl chopped up in the refrigerator to munch at work.

Preparation is key to sticking with this for 90 days. Always keep chopped vegetables and whole fruits available.

When you make one of the great menus at the back of this book, separate leftovers as servings to microwave later so that you always have something quick on hand. When healthy food is available we don't eat what we shouldn't.

Breakfast is usually fruit and *always* proceeded by a glass of ice water. Ice water first thing in the morning jolts your metabolism to life and prepares your body to wash out what has been sitting inside it all night.

Fruit has fiber to aid in digestion. It scrubs through you taking waste with it and it fills you up. Fruit is loaded with vitamins and it tastes good.

Lunch is soup and/or a salad. The middle of the day is when we do most of our work or play. Eating something filling AND light keeps us feeling our best and diminishes the urge to visit the kitchen.

Dinner is for socializing or relaxing with our hobbies. At dinner we get nutrients we may not have had earlier. The recipes in the back of the book are a start, alter them to your taste and look online for new ones. (You can find tips and new recipes every week at **bodymindsoulmoney.com**)

Get at least a half of a cup of beans *with* ¼ cup barley, or brown rice daily. (White rice is processed food, don't eat it.) OR just half a cup of cooked quinoa every day. Quinoa, like meat, is a complete protein on its own, brown rice combined with beans is a complete protein as well.
You need protein every day!

Veggies you **should** eat anytime with no consequences:

Celery, lettuce, kale, green beans, spinach, zucchini, mushrooms, green pepper, cucumbers, tomato, broccoli, plain potato, cauliflower, asparagus, carrots and **artichokes.**

Fruits you should eat are:
Peaches, pears, apples, berries, cantaloupe, plums, nectarine, mangos, persimmons, apricots and cherries.

Flavorings include:
Vinegars, lemon, lime, garlic, onion, herbs and spices, (we love Mrs. Dash) unsweetened cocoa, and **salt alternatives.**

Spices like **cinnamon, ginger, turmeric *with black pepper*, cayenne** and **garlic** are anti-inflammatory and taken daily increase the speed of weight loss. Herbs like **cilantro** and **parsley** bind with toxins and remove them from your body.

Foods you **can** eat after or with the above:

Bananas, oranges, pumpkin, yams, corn, pineapple, avocado, and **almond milk. Coconut milk, nuts, raisins** and **maple syrup** should only be used in moderation.

Foods you **should not** eat for 90 days:

Meat, seafood, eggs, dairy products, animal products, (bone broth, gelatin, honey, cricket flour, Soylent-Green) butter, flour, sugar, oils, salt, non-dairy creamers, diet soda, aspartame, sucralose and **maltodextrin.**

I am on the fence about **saccharin**, but it's the only artificial sweetener I'd use.

Honey is technically an animal product. It's also loaded with its own kind of sugar. If you really need it in your tea or coffee, have just a little. Maple syrup is better, also used in moderation.

Speaking of drinks, **green tea** boosts metabolism, **white tea** stunts fat cells, **black tea** and **orange tea** -with a little cinnamon- suppresses appetite, **herb tea** sooths you to sleep and **cold** they are all ways to get **ice water** if you don't enjoy drinking water.

Scan and print the preceding page and tape it to your refrigerator or inside a cupboard door to refer to daily.

Now, you know about this new way of eating, let's get started on changing the rest of your life.

Day #1

Be Grateful

You have decided to make big changes. Congratulations on your motivation.

Before we begin, it is essential that you appreciate *who* and *where you are now*. This is your "before" and it took all your life to get here.

What positive aspects do you have that you can build on?

Unless you pirated this book, you have a little money, you bought it (or your computer or e-reader). You have assets!

You're reading this so you have a basic education. As of this printing one sixth of adults in the world are still functionally illiterate, and you can read.

You are at least relatively healthy. You have a good body. Maybe it's not perfect, but it works!

You have the basics under control! Be grateful.

Count the assets you have above those basics be happy that you are where you are right now; it's a great place to start but you can have so much more!

Now let's tap into your deeper potential!
You've read this far, you've made a start. I'm grateful.

Good luck.

Meditation: *Please help me to be grateful for what I have already received. I will strive for what I want to achieve with compassion for others, a positive attitude and strength for myself, my family, and my world.*

Body:

Take Inventory

Weigh yourself. Measure your neck, upper and forearms, waist, legs and hips. Take pictures, blog and/or update the chart!
Drink your first glass of water when you wake up and your last glass of ice water before 7:30 and have nothing more.
Try to avoid eating after 7:00 to promote proper digestion and prevent heartburn. It may even help you sleep better.

Money:

Make a video or a list of your property. Include cash, real estate, vehicles, rentals, investments, insurance policies, electronics, jewelry and appliances. Date it and keep in a safe place in case you need it for insurance or legal purposes.

Mind:

Start each day with exercise for your body *and for your mind*: Memorize a joke each morning and <u>tell the joke</u> when the opportunity arises! Telling jokes builds verbal acuity and confidence. People may groan sometimes, but they will soon look forward to your daily moment of levity.

Run your finger over the joke of the day or recite it to yourself a few times to fix it in your brain three different ways.

Joke:
Today I learned "Wet Floor" signs are not a request.

Day #2

Be Aware

You have probably heard the phrase "God is in the details." It's true. One look into the complex structure of a dandelion will tell you that for us to replicate it is impossible. The intricate details that go into everything in nature are astounding and we forget to notice them.

All around us are miracles, when we notice and point them out to others we get a heightened awareness of our place in the world.

Too often we go through our days oblivious to many sights, sounds, smells and textures that would delight us if we took the time to notice them.

Try to describe the sound of wind chimes. It changes with every breeze. A chime can make you aware of a breeze that may carry the scent of roses, cotton candy, barbeque, or cologne.

Stop and take a few seconds out of each day to see, smell, feel, and hear the things around you. Notice the scent of your family or coworkers as they walk by. Really feel your food on your tongue and pick out the nuances of the flavors. Think about how you would tell someone about an interesting color you may see. You will soon be able to remember the sights, sounds, smells and temperatures that you consciously gather and use them when you need them.

If you can describe your day to a friend in a way that will capture their attention you can take them to that moment.

For instance, a traffic jam is stressful if you can re-experience your favorite piece of art or the smell of the county fair.

As a bonus to your new awareness, misunderstandings about the past will end quickly. You'll be able to put the other person back in the moment by relating the exact circumstances, words and inflections of a time in question.

Meditation: *Please help me notice the miraculous things around me. I will carry those things with me as treasure to spend in moments when I need them.*

Body:
Stretch your muscles consciously before getting out of bed, before standing, after long periods of work, or extended periods of inactivity. It prevents cramps, pulled muscles, and helps you keep your balance when standing.

Money:
Count and wrap loose coins, smooth out crumpled bills and arrange them in the same direction. Learn to respect money. Save all of your change and deposit it each Friday, even if it's just $5.00 in a credit union account. Soon you will have "extra" money for investments then your money works for you!

Mind:
Look around the room then close your eyes and list everything you saw. No peeking. Are you surprised by the things you didn't remember? Try it again. Remember more? Do this daily to train yourself as a trusted observer. It's a skill most people don't develop.

Joke:
"One man's raison d'etre is another man's Plan Be."

Day #3

Be Empathetic

Molly was nearly done shopping when her two-year-old threw her very first public fit. She threw herself to the floor screaming, leaving Molly holding her newborn and searching her purse for her debit card to pay for her groceries and get out of there.

A woman frowned and said. "I swear my kids would never have gotten away with that."

Molly glanced up at her, fumbled and dropped her card, when she bent to retrieve it, she hit her head on the cart on the way down and then her baby's head on the way up. Now she had two crying babies and she wanted to cry herself. Instead, she yelled at her toddler to pacify the mean lady. The little girl cried louder. She finally paid for her groceries and left, embarrassed and angry at herself.

Imagine how much better everyone would have felt if someone had stepped in to help the young mother.

Outside of placing the child in a soundproof box, what could you do to make things easier? For one thing, maybe not criticize.

You were once a kid and you probably were tired, hungry, ignored or unhappy. *The mean woman was obviously throwing her own version of a fit for those very reasons.*

Put yourself in the child's place but don't forget to put yourself in the mother's place too, look to her first and make sure she knows you are willing to help and never touch a child without permission.

Learning to deal with people of all ages is a matter of putting yourself in their place.

Meditation: *Please help me to remember that what I criticize in others I may have experienced myself. Give me the wisdom to do what I would want done for me.*

Body:

Close your doors draw the drapes and dance all the way through a song as if you are in a club and people are watching.

Dancing not only burns calories, it raises your metabolism so that even when you are still, your body will burn fat and food. Dancing helps with stamina, balance and coordination. You'll be stronger more graceful and agile.

Two left feet? Fix that. You can find instructional videos online or at your local library. Learning to dance opens up new social opportunities and impresses people at weddings, clubs and parties. Also, it's fun.

Money:

Buy groceries for an entire month if you can. Reducing trips to the store saves on gas and impulse buys. Milk and bread can be frozen and thawed as you need them. Eggs will last a month.

Mind:

Round all prices to the nearest dollar as you shop and add each item to a running total in your head or on your phone. You won't go over your budget.

Joke:
"Whoever invented those counterfeit-detecting pens
was write on the money."

Day #4

Meditate or Pray

When is the last time you took fifteen minutes to think about nothing? Have you ever done that?
When is the last time you watched a video just because it was on? Maybe *nothing* would have been better. In fact, it would have.

Studies have shown that people who deliberately take fifteen minutes a day to concentrate on *not thinking* actually think more clearly for several hours afterward!

Forget the image you may have of a yogi sitting on a mountain in a lotus position chanting, "Ohm." Meditating is as simple as sitting in a quiet spot and staring at a spot on the wall.

If you have a comfortable chair lean back in it and clear your mind of all thoughts. Thoughts will try to sneak in. You can chase them out by thinking of yourself sitting in a big, soft, white cartoon bubble.

If you choose to pray instead, talk to your God about all that is right in your world and be thankful.

It is important that you spend the whole fifteen minutes alone without too many sounds. If you can't find a quiet spot, turn on instrumental music to block distractions.

Even if it seems ridiculous to you, try it for just one week. If you don't find yourself calmer and better able to handle everyday pressure you can go back to reruns of "Friends".

Meditation: *Please help me clear my mind of thoughts and feelings that get in the way of concentration and productivity. I will think of positive images and activities to replace those of despair and weakness when my mind is clear and open.*

Body:

Schedule a haircut or trim.

(If you cut your own hair, now is the time to do it. If you're not experienced, leave it to the professionals.)

Consider a new style and find one you like in a magazine or online! You don't have to go to extremes but change is good, you're changing everything about yourself!

Each time you see your new cut in the mirror you will be reminded that you are on your way to your goals!

Money:

Write a list of your payments. Utilities, mortgage, credit cards, loans, taxes, child support, gas, groceries, repairs etc. Prioritize the list. Can you negotiate a lower interest rate? Which can you pay off? Which can you consolidate?

Mind:

Every day, clear your mind of thoughts and concentrate on the sound and feeling of your breath. Do this for ten to fifteen minutes. Try not to even think about your breath. Clearing your mind clears the cobwebs, allowing your thoughts to run without interference! With practice you can meditate anywhere.

Joke:
"The flat earth society has members all around the globe."

Day #5

Simplify Your Day

The alarm goes off. If you are like many people and it's a weekday, you set your ordinary day in motion. You:

> Roll out of bed, shower, brush your teeth, do your make-up or shave/trim your beard and moustache, blow dry/style hair or shave head, choose clothing, iron wrinkly items, dress, accessorize, make your bed, eat breakfast, check your agenda/appointments, help get your housemates (kids, spouse, animals) ready for their day, do anything important from the day before, (permission slips, newsletters) go to work, check email, make phone calls, do your actual job, order birthday, anniversary, Secretary's Day, Sweetest Day, Mother's day, Father's Day, Grandparent's Day, National Hamburger Day, (Seriously, do we need that?) Christmas, or graduation cards and/or presents, do co-workers/boss/ subordinates undone parts of your projects, organize your work area, fight traffic, pick up kids, gas your car, catch up on errands like picking up prescriptions and dry-cleaning, make/buy dinner, clean up after dinner, do dishes, do laundry, do housework, help with homework, counsel your mate/kids as they talk about their stressful day, brush the dog/cat/fuzzy slipper, (who knows at this point?) watch television, read a book or magazine or surf the web, brush your teeth, brush your hair, put on body/foot/face cream, dress in night clothes, hit the rack, have sex (if you still have the energy) and then finally, *sleep.*

Tomorrow you will get up and do it again, praying for the weekend so you can do things that you want to do. Do you sometimes feel you have a crank in your back and you are a machine that does the same thing over and over and over?

What can you do to break off that winding crank and live the way you want to live?

Do you need that perfect makeup? Choose just a few easy to apply products. Do you need that finely trimmed beard? Buy an electric trimmer.

Save time by combing your hair and letting it air-dry or braid long hair instead of blowing and styling.

Simplify choosing your clothing by buying solid colored clothing and separates that go well together. Ditch clothes that need ironing more than a few times a year. (Steve Jobs only wore jeans and a black t-shirt to save time and aggravation. Johnny Cash only wore black.)

Your six-year-old can make her own bed and a simple breakfast. Older kids can help younger ones. Does your spouse have extra time to lend a hand? Delegate.

Can you send your kids to school with other parents sometimes? (You must reciprocate obviously.)

Fill your tank instead of getting a partial tank to save wasteful trips to the gas station and the urge to buy junk food.

Toughening up on delegating tasks at work can make a huge difference. You should only have to do YOUR job.

Older children can help with homework, in exchange for a "tutoring fee". Good work habits start at home.

All kids can help cook and clean.

Subscription gifting services make holidays easier.

Calling your significant other on your lunch break for just ten minutes when you both have time helps you catch up and stay close. It also saves time you can spend with kids or friends later and brightens your day like only someone who loves you can.

Buy frozen family meals, use a crock pot, or order in to save dinner time stress.

Sleep naked to save time, laundry and develop closeness with your mate or just enjoy the sensation.

Find things you can do now to save time later to free up time to relax away from your schedule.

When you cut out unnecessary things from your day you leave time to *enjoy* your life. Use the extra time to get to know your son's girlfriend, take your dog for a longer walk, plan a vacation, or catch up on sleep!

Meditation: *Please help me to weed out the things that distract me from living my life to its fullest. I will remember to use my extra time wisely and enjoy the moments I spend doing what I want to do.*

Body:

Walk or exercise in comfortable clothes if you can. It is a form of meditation on its own. If you are self-conscious exercising in front of other people, wear loose clothes but remember, most people feel just like you do, they may be worried about what *you* are thinking of them!
(Be careful not to wear clothes that will snag on bicycle chains, exercise equipment or weeds.)

As you lose pounds you will want to wear more form-fitting clothes to show off your new body. Also, your old clothes will no longer fit.

Money:

For one week, write down everything you buy, even a pack of gum. At the end of the week you will be surprised at how things add up!   What can you live without or buy generic?

Mind:

Set a learning goal. What would you like to learn in the next 85 days? You could learn the basics of a language, complete a computer training program, learn to play bridge, write the first draft of a book, or paint a masterpiece!

Joke:
"A recent study has found out that people who carry a little extra weight live longer than people who mention it."

Day #6

Look for Beauty in All People

There is indescribable beauty inside some very unremarkable people. The secret to unlocking it is to get to know the person.

Contemporaries of Vincent Van Gogh described him as "not attractive" and "a bit unsociable" with "a vicious character". Yet Van Gogh produced beautiful art and was capable of great generosity.

One bitterly cold winter, Van Gogh encountered a sick and pregnant woman prostituting herself to stay alive. He took her into his home, shared his meager amount of food with her and paid her all he could afford to model for his paintings. She in turn gave him companionship through the winter and some of the beautiful images that we see in museums to this day.

A misfit himself, Van Gogh saw beauty in a cast-off woman and used that insight to create priceless art!

You probably see people every day that you don't find attractive. If you took the time to get to know them you might find that the unfriendly man three doors down, is a shy tenor for the local opera, or that the homeless woman who asks for change donates half of it to a local animal shelter.

You don't have to form a friendship bond with someone to show them kindness and see what gifts their life holds for you. Just get to know them. It never hurts to have another friend.

Meditation: *Please help me to remember that there is more than meets the eye in people I encounter. Give me courage to explore and accept unusual people I meet.*

Body:

Are you keeping up? Day six is the hardest day. It's almost a week and those who fear success (or lack of success) will have second thoughts about continuing. Those week one numbers are nothing to be afraid of. You may be surprised. If not, there's no harm in starting again!

To motivate yourself, get down on the floor right now and do five push-ups!

When the idea of quitting enters your head, chase it out with the good hormones that movement gives you. The feeling of accomplishment you get when you take action will spill over into your professional and personal life too. You may find you procrastinate less often!

Money:

Give money to charity. When you donate, you give away the tendency to be greedy. This helps you spend and invest wisely instead of holding on or taking stupid risks.

Mind:

Research how money is delegated from your local charities. If a lot of administrative costs are involved, choose another charity to make your money matter.

Joke:
A convincing stick-on moustache is a hard thing to pull off.

Day #7

Be Humble

You have already changed one week of your life for the better. You have learned six good moral lessons and have gotten closer to your goal of being mindful.

Before you celebrate, remember, whatever you do, don't do it not for praise but because you want to be a better person.

As your face shape changes, as it will as you lose weight, and your body gets slender, flatterers may fill your head with the idea that you are becoming superior to others. Conversely, some people may try to derail your accomplishments by saying you aren't the person you used to be. (Isn't that the goal?) They just fear change. Assure them that you love them and are not trying to grow away, only up. Maybe they will join you.

Be aware of this possibility and know that regardless of what anyone says, you are changing for the better. You can look forward to eleven more weeks of new ideas, body transforming food, and guidance to get you closer to the intelligent, caring, beautiful person you have always been inside.

You will get to your ultimate goal and when you do, you will find that although you are a better person you are not better than anyone else, just the best you can be.

Meditation: *Please help me to recognize my accomplishments without fanfare. I earn the recognition but the only one I really need to impress is myself.*

Body:

It's the end of week one!
Time to take a new inventory.
Every week you will weigh yourself, measure your neck, chest, arms, waist, legs and hips and write your results on the chart at the end of the book. Take pictures, blog and/or update the chart.
A week's worth of progress might not seem like a lot now, but it shows what you can do! It's ok that other people don't know about your progress and plans, they will soon notice you're looking better and achieving more.

Achievement multiplies. Keep up the good work!

Money:

Take free music lessons, tax preparation courses, or photography classes at home. You can learn at college level through online courses. Test out of those classes later and save money on college.

Mind:

Locate a facility or web site that can help you with your goal. MIT offers free classes online but no credit for those classes. However, other colleges offer credit by testing your knowledge on those subjects. You can also just learn to juggle, sew, or play guitar. Learn for YOU!

Joke:
"When you keep horses, your life is more stable."

Day #8

Notice the Changes

You have already seen changes in your first week of this program; you are probably a few pounds lighter and a few experiences wiser.

If you stick with it, this program will bring about big changes. Clothes will begin to outgrow you. New clothes will start to fit you. Some friends who refuse to change or accept your will feel left behind, (and that is for the better) some may seize your example and change their own lives, and new people and situations will come to influence you in positive ways.

Look around you. What else has changed in this week of your life? Has anyone gotten a haircut, a cool shirt, started smiling at you more than usual?

Look for the changes and notice the opportunities that come along with them. Use those opportunities to create more changes. Mentioning that new shirt or haircut might be an opportunity to network with a new person. Watch how fast paying attention helps you succeed in your social life!

Changes take us forward. With each change, there is an opportunity to make another one. That's progress that leads to evolution.

Just as good grades on a test make it possible for us to learn the next lesson, a good experience opens us up to a better one.

Meditation: *Please help me to recognize that changes allow me to evolve. I will use those changes to make better choices and move forward on my path.*

__Body:__

Check your supplies. Do you have vitamins, lotion, aspirin? Do you have workout clothes? Do you need hand weights or a gym equipment?
Look for bikes at yard sales and thrift shops. Ask friends if they have an old bike they don't use. You may be doing them a favor by freeing up their garage space.

You can often find FREE gym equipment online or on community Facebook pages.

__Money:__

You would be surprised at how much money you may have lying around your house. Do a cash safari right now and collect every dime and nickel from jackets, pants, dresser tops, laundry rooms and even your couch. Remember to deposit all the change you find every week, even if it is just $5. Watch it add up!

__Mind:__

Use your down-time wisely. Instead of smoking a cigarette (please quit) or seeking snacks, write a diary entry. A diary in your handwriting will be entertaining to read in the years ahead and can be used as a legal record if you ever need it.

Joke:
"Microscopes allow us to enjoy the little things in life."

Day #9

"Notice Doublespeak"

The time has come to start looking outside of your thoughts and into those who influence you:

Whether you know it or not you are being bombarded by other people's thoughts in a negative way.

If you click through stations on your radio, you may hear a talk-radio host's tough, angry talk, and you will definitely hear politicians telling you to be afraid.

The talk radio host often condemns other who share his vices. Politicians will reveal their own weakness by accusing their opponents of it.

Our leaders use *fear* in times of *safety* to get us to change our minds about something they want to own or control.

Be aware of the phenomena of "doublespeak" a term used in George Orwell's *1984* that means language constructed deliberately to disguise or distort its actual meaning.

Awareness means recognizing that words like "alternative facts" mean "lies" and "small business" means "large corporations". "Fake news" is often true.

It also will help us understand that someone we call an "insurgent" is another country's patriot.

Deception isn't always verbal. Listen for tone and cadence, to realize their bullying techniques.

Meditation: *Please help me recognize deception and make up my own mind. I won't be fooled by people whose objectives conflict with my own.*

Body:

Pay attention to your energy level, is it increasing or decreasing? If it is decreasing, you may be working too hard. If you know that's not the case, see your doctor and ask for tests for anemia or thyroid.

You may find you're tuning into your circadian rhythm. You may have more energy in the morning or in the afternoon. Once you discover your pattern, you can adjust your schedule and get more done when you are most energetic.

Your stamina should be increasing, if it's not adjust your carbohydrates up or your exercise down.

Money:

Ignore "get rich quick" schemes. More often than not the authors who sell you those products made their money not through what they are telling you but by selling the product they are selling you!

Mind:

Read Orwell's 1984. Do you think it was a prediction or do you think his fiction gave our leaders ideas?
What do you think the future will look like? How can you shape it?

Joke:
Where would we be without rhetorical questions?

Day #10

Listen to Rival Views

You know enough to listen for the ring of truth in broadcast media and you recognize the language that can cue you in to biases.

Now listen to those biases. Try to understand their motives.

You don't have to subscribe to their school of thought, but when you listen to people with opposing ideas, you may find that you share some of those views.

A fourteen-year-old rape victim's stepfather forced her to get an abortion. The story spread through the church.
The following Sunday, the girl had to sit through a sermon condemning the horrible sins of women who would callously kill their own "babies". The child attempted suicide and when her pastor sat with her in the hospital she very bravely told him the whole story.

The step-father was the father of the fetus he had forced her to abort. He was arrested and the young pastor gave a revised speech the next Sunday. He had never personally known anyone who had been raped or had lived through an abortion. He was merely uttering what he had been taught at seminary.

That girl, now a mother, works at an adoption agency helping women find homes for babies they can't raise.

The pastor holds group counseling sessions for women who have had abortions.

Both took their positions because of someone who had an opposing view on a complicated subject.
Listen to your enemies, you might find a way to use their experiences to help someone.

Meditation: *Please help me to try to understand ideas with which I don't agree in order to better understand people I might meet. I will listen to views that differ from my own with an open mind.*

Body:

While sitting, breathe in for ten seconds and out for ten seconds. Try it once an hour. Fresh air gives you energy! When you expand your lung capacity, you expand your access to oxygen. Oxygen burns fat.

As you breathe deeply aware of your stomach muscles, allow them to expand with each breath and contract them with each exhale. It's a two-for-one exercise!

Money:

If you deserve a raise, gently ask for it with examples of your value. No company wants to lose a good employee. In order to be taken seriously, know what your response will be to "no" and be prepared to follow through.

Mind:

Using your non-dominate hand helps you think differently. Spend five minutes every day writing with the hand you don't normally use. (Maybe for your to-do list!)

Joke:
"My blind date didn't see anything in me"

Day #11
Don't Force Change

Have you ever seen what happens when someone tries to fill a water balloon with high velocity water pressure?

The balloon will do one of two things, it will fly off the spout and have to be recovered and repositioned, or it will burst. Either way, that balloon was not the fun-bomb you planned and in one case, it's ruined!

It's the same thing with life changes. If you try to do too much all at once, one of two things will happen; you will get burnt out and quit, (flying off the spout) or you will injure yourself (ruin your progress).

You must respect what your body is telling you. If you are uncomfortable walking a mile, walk a half mile. If you feel nauseous when you smell asparagus, eat green beans. Don't push yourself too hard.

On "Worldwide 24-Hour Comics Day" a few years ago a man tried to beat his record of 24 pages in 18 hours. He sketched, wrote, colored and drew ferociously and didn't even come close to beating his own time.

Since that day he hasn't drawn one page. He says his mind hurts. No small wonder; he was using his right hand and his left brain at a breakneck speed for 18 hours straight. It's now gone on strike for better working conditions! He no longer loves to draw comics.

When you force change, it will fight back.
Use this book as a guide. It is designed for quick results but *was not meant to be followed exactly.*

If you need a chocolate chip cookie, eat one. (only one please) If your legs hurt from yesterday, DO NOT stress them today.

Meditation: *Please help me realize that some limits are there to protect me. I will recognize when I'm endangering myself and slow down to sustain my inertia.*

__Body:__

While sitting stretch your neck to the left and right then down to your chest while breathing deeply. (Not backward.) This is a stress fighter that also fights neck flab!
It's never a good idea to force your neck backward.
The bones of your neck were not designed to move that way and it could cause an injury or pinched nerve.

Your arms and legs benefit from flexibility gained from stretching them a little further, your neck is not like that, be careful with it to avoid injury.

__Money:__

To save an average of $750 a year, *quit the gym. S*ee if your local college or high school has open gym hours. Sometimes you can pay as little as $2 a visit!
Look for exercises online that don't require equipment or buy used equipment online…then use it.

__Mind:__

Writing notes in the margins of your books as you read them is a great exercise that helps retain knowledge and improves recall! (Only do this if you *own* a paper copy of the book!)

Joke:
"I'm against protesting, but I don't know how to show it."

Day #12

Be Aware of Desires

Your neighbor just pulled up in his new car. It's a beauty with all the options. He built his house two years ago and he's having it remodeled. He's carrying pictures from his trip to Europe, and are those shoes *Italian*?

Your shoes came from a discount store, that rattle trap in your driveway needs new brakes. Your last vacation was spent fixing cracks in your garage wall.
He's such a creep, why is he always showing off?
Why can't you have all of that?

Maybe it's time to check your priorities. Why do you desire those things?
Your car is the perfect size for your family and you never have to panic when the baby spills a drink.
Europe? No. You love camping.
What about the historic beauty of the home you have worked so hard to preserve? Many people envy that.

There are times when we all want to be the one who has it all, but if we contemplate our true desires we might find we already have everything we need.

One look below the surface of your neighbor's possessions might reveal a miserable man. That new car has just put him $30,000 in debt. The remodel might be because inferior building materials in newer houses require more maintenance. He may have taken his wife to Europe keep her away from the lover that keeps her company while he works 60-hour weeks to pay for what he owns, including those Italian shoes.

Do you want to *look* happy or to be happy?

Make a list of your absolute essentials according to priority. How many of them do you already have? Which are the most important? What would it take to get them all? Will they really make you happy?

Meditation: *Please help me to realize that those things that I desire may exact a price on my happiness. I will be aware of my desires and the reasons behind them.*

Body:

Walk a little further than you normally do. (You should be walking at least a half mile a day.
Can you do a mile? If you can do it.
If you can't walk in your neighborhood, walk in your yard, building or parking lot. If you can't get outside, walk around your house. Use your stairs! 2000 steps is a mile.

If you can't or choose not to walk, exercise your upper body.

Money:

Never buy anything that you don't really need. Why buy a whole collection of scented candles when you only burn a few? What can be "new to them" from your own closet?

Mind:

Use crazy sounding pegs to help you remember names. Don Jabitsky can be remembered by thinking of a sunrise in which a Rasta-god with Don's face is biting a very colorful cloud. "At dawn, Jah bit the sky." Don Jah-bit-sky He might wonder why you smile each you see him.

Joke:
"Even a screw-up can install a light bulb."

Day #13

Lose What You Don't Need

I came home with groceries one day to realize that there was no place to put the bags on my counter.

I pushed the blender back against the wall, put the lid on the food processor and pushed it up against the stand mixer, between the smoothie machine and the toaster, then picked up the chop mincer, rinsed the nuts out of it and bent down to put it in a cabinet.

As I was looking for a place for it among the crowded shelves I noticed a juicer that had not been used for three years, a blender that I only use for parties, two counter-top press grills, two waffle makers, a mini donut machine, an air popcorn popper AND an oil popper, a slicer, two hand-mixers, a wok and a nice crock pot, a gift received many years ago, still in the box.

I put the groceries away then placed everything except the food processor, toaster, and stand mixer into a box. I put that box in my basement and marked it "extra appliances".

That was two years ago. I only opened it once for a countertop grill that I later returned to the box.

When a pipe began to leak in my basement I brought the box up. For a moment I was tempted to put some of those things back in the cabinet, but I realized that not once in two years have I had to clear a spot for groceries or rearrange my cabinets.

My life was better because I didn't have those extra appliances. I did buy a new blender; a used Vita-mix I always wanted. (I use it every day.) There was plenty of space for it.

That was an epiphany. I cleared out my office and lost 6 more items. My printer does many things so I got rid of my ancient fax machine, tank-sized copier, and flatbed scanner. I tossed two staplers and an extra shredder out as well.
Now I can make a guest comfortable in my office. I have a comfy table and chair where the supply shelf stood!

On a more personal level, I was reminded of people that have come and gone in my life. Some were destructive, (alcoholic drinking buddies) some were demanding (jealous and clingy friends) and some took a lot of my time but gave nothing in return. (energy vampires)

There were also those people who just made me feel uncomfortable when they were around, no real reason. We just didn't click. They were like those appliances. They were there for years, but I didn't know why.

They took up space in my life that I didn't know I needed. I made a list of people I can't live without and made an effort to contact them and let them know they were on my mind. (I put them on my countertop.)

I have now consciously surrounded myself with people who stimulate and encourage me.

I did not offend, reject or completely dispose of the people who were inert, I like to help people, and they often give me a chance to do that.

I no longer accept invitations nor extend invitations to people who are harmful to me or my loved ones. (I put them in the box) I may invite them back one day. I hold no malice toward them. I hope they feel the same.

I have no doubt their lives have improved because they have more time to spend with people whose interests match their own.

I spend more time with people who make me happy and I look for ways to make them happy. I call them if I can't see them, and I have time to listen to what they want to say. There is space in my life for potential new friends. My life is better because I cleared out what was in my way.

Meditation: *Please help me to wisely sort out the things I don't need in my life like old clothes and other things I never use, and also people who harm me or don't deserve my time. I will decide carefully if something or someone is necessary and helpful before allowing them into my life.*

Body:

Reminder! Practice **WISDOM.**
Walk at least half a mile. Isometrically contract your muscles. Shower in cool water. Drink ice water. Open your lungs and breathe. Move when you can.

This might be a good time to try on new combinations of clothes you usually don't wear. Your clothes should fit better now and you might feel like you are shopping in your own closet.
Donate what you will never wear or sell them at consignment shops or at a tag sale.

Money:

Use Ebay.com to sell unneeded household items; Amazon to sell used books; and Craigslist to sell cars and houses. The price is low (Craigslist is free) and people check them every day!

Mind:

Get rid of clutter on your desk to be more productive.
Get rid of clutter in your home to stay calm.
Clutter forces us to spend time rearranging things or thinking "I should clean this." or "What's this doing here?" instead of concentrating on more important things.

Joke:
I may have a bad memory but at least
I don't have a bad memory.

Day #14

Listen More Than You Talk

Sara was always interrupting. Her friends would tell each other this joke:

"Knock. Knock."
"Who's there?"
"Interrupting cow."
"Interrupting cow wh…"
"Sara!"

She overheard the mean joke and was crushed. She asked a friend if it was true and before he could finish, she interrupted! He said "Sara, just please <u>listen</u>!"

Sara, feeling indignant showed up at his party wearing duct tape on her mouth with the words, "Just Listening." printed on it. It backfired in the best way. She got a few laughs and kept it on all night. She wandered from room to room, listening to conversations, nodding or shaking her head to communicate.

She learned that one of her friends was having a baby and another was divorcing. She heard details that she never would have known if she had been the one talking. She made up her mind to consciously listen and grew much closer to her friends as a result.

Sara is an entertainer. She leaves no dead air in conversations.

She thinks ahead so people don't get bored. (People know when we aren't listening and get bored anyway.)

Sara has worked hard to kick her interrupting habit and develop a better view of herself. She knows that her friends love her and that a lull in conversation doesn't mean she isn't witty or fun, "Just Listening."

Meditation: *Please give my ears the pleasure of someone else's words and my mind the ability to learn from them.*

Body:

It's been 2 weeks!
Weigh yourself. Measure your neck, chest, arms, waist, legs and hips. Take pictures, blog and/or update the chart!

Don't worry if your weight loss has started to slow down. Your increased movement and gentle exercise is building muscle. Muscle weighs more than fat but helps you look thinner and burn fat more efficiently.
Your weight loss might not be as fast now, but it will be steady, healthy and more permanent!

Money:

Join your local chamber of commerce to network with the greatest minds in your town. It can improve your cash flow as you may hear of new opportunities before anyone else.

Mind:

Spend more time with intelligent people. We become like the people with whom we associate. Unfortunately, the opposite is also true. Spend time with idiots to become one.
Joke:
I've got a fear of speed bumps, but I'm slowly getting over it.

Day #15

Stay With Your Goal

We have all set certain goals for ourselves. For some it is as simple as getting a summer job. For others, it is as complicated as attaining a regional manager position within five years.

Sometimes after applying for and being denied a few jobs it is tempting to quit and spend the summer on the couch instead. Or after being passed over for the manager position twice, just to pray for your supervisor's demise!

However, if you keep plugging away you may find that the seventh place you apply is the one with the highest wage and the best co-workers. If you research you may find you are more than qualified to fill the regional manager position for your company's *rival*!

Unless your goal is to be the CEO of a Fortune 500 company and you just finished high school, you have a chance. (Even then, why not try, it is possible.)

The most important thing you need to achieve anything, is a *goal*. The second most important thing is the stamina to stick with it and look for the opportunities that will present themselves along the way. Some opportunities may change your goals, and some may get you to it sooner!

It's been said that the only man who truly loses is the man who does not try. I would go one further and say *he who quits trying* loses more.

Meditation: *Please help me to not lose sight of the end of the race. I will run on the track even as it changes because I know there is a reward at the finish line.*

Body:

While sitting, raise your ankles up to the height of your knees. Repeat 10 times to tighten saggy knees and improve circulation to your legs.

The muscles around your knees do more than bend with every step. They help you keep your balance and absorb that initial burst of speed when you want to run. A tear in a knee ligament may require surgery and will knock you down for weeks. Strengthening knee muscles keeps ligaments strong and ready when you need them.

Money:

Set a money goal and write it down. "I'd like to have $100,000 in the bank by January of next year." Tuck it in your wallet. Sounds crazy but it will help you keep your eyes open for ways to get there!

Mind:

Before you sleep, think of the things you have to do tomorrow. Imagine yourself doing them effortlessly. You may be surprised at what a great next day you have!

Joke:
"I didn't want to have the organ transplant at first,
but then I had a change of heart."

Day #16

Find Other Ways to Get There

Two roads diverged in a wood, and I—
I took the one less traveled by,
And that has made all the difference.
-Robert Frost

Janet lived in a small apartment and rode her bicycle to work each day down a path along a river. Every day she saw people kayaking and thought, "I wish I could afford a place to keep a kayak."
On weekends, she rented a kayak and explored places she had never been. When she returned it one afternoon she overheard some men talking about how they needed a quiet place to film along the river. Janet told the men about two easily accessible places and offered to show them where they were.

On the trip back, one of the men dumped his kayak and Janet helped him right it, told him what he had done wrong and how to correct it.

When they returned to the rental place the man who dumped his kayak took her to the owner of the company and said. "Here's your manager."
It turns out the company also owns an adventure tour company and was looking for someone to manage a new location.
The day's filming was a promotional video for the company. Janet was in the right place at the right time.

Her new job not only afforded her an apartment big enough to keep a kayak, but opportunities to use it.

Whatever you want, there is a way to get it if you keep your mind open to alternate possibilities.

Meditation: *Please help me recognize chances presented to me. I will keep my mind open to new possibilities.*

Body:

With your arms to your sides and your thumbs in, push your fist down and back as far behind you as is comfortable.
Repeat on both side ten to twenty times. This shrinks those bat wings and tightens shoulders.
When you do stretching exercises of any kind, it pays to be aware of how far your body wants to move.
If it hurts, don't do it. If you feel something unusual, stop whatever it is you are doing and relax.
Your body is getting stronger and more flexible. An injury would be a set-back at this point.

Money:

Love to spend time out on the water but can't afford a boat? Offer to clean boats in exchange for time on the water! You don't have to own what you want to use!

Mind:

How many ways can you think of to do what you love?
List your hobbies and think of other ways to do them!

Joke:
Penultimate is my second least favorite word.

Day #17

Status is Worth Less Than Satisfaction

I was talking to my doctor about my friend who, after years of working at a desk and being downsized had found a new joy in working outdoors for a road crew.

She told me she had a patient who had worked most of his life in management and when his firm went under, he found himself unemployed and over 50. His job prospects were slim so he took a temporary job working with a friend as a groundskeeper for a local college.

She said to her amazement his blood pressure dropped and she took him off medication. Arthritis that he had in his "phone hand" was suddenly gone and every single time she saw him he had a smile on his face.

She asked if he told people he worked as a gardener and he said "At first I was vague, but it made me feel guilty, like I was saying I was ashamed of my job. I love my job. Now when people ask me what I do I say, "I put the 'green' in Bowling Green!"

He had learned that it doesn't matter what people think of what you do. He loved his job and did it well. His health and happiness were all that mattered.

Meditation: *Please help me to understand that if I do the best I can, I will be happy no matter what the position. I will seek to "grow where I'm planted".*

Body:

While sitting, stretch your upper body muscles slowly, as far to the right and then the left as is comfortable. This is great for your waist and back.

You can do this while standing too, being careful to keep your lower body stationary and not to swing your body wildly, which can cause injury.

Always be aware of your spine, never stretch or twist it to a point where you feel discomfort.

To add more muscle-power stretch your hands and arms too!

Money:

Name brand products costs up to 3X more than store brands. Sometimes the only difference is the box! Save hundreds of dollars a year by buying store brands or generic products.

Mind:

While doing grunt work, people often get their best ideas. The dishwasher was invented by someone who hated washing dishes! What inventions would make your life better?
As you go through your day think of ways to make it easier. You may be the next great inventor!

Joke:
If you are cold, sit in the corner, it's 90 degrees.

Day #18

Get Educated

Calista and Carrie went to the same college. Calista dropped out in her second year. She had seen enough and was tired of having no money to spend. She took a job in the office of a local factory, did her eight hours, paid her bills and looked forward to the weekend.

Carrie struggled to finish her degree. In her final year, her college offered a placement service. One position in her town offered a great salary with benefits that Carrie couldn't pass up. She applied for and got the job.

Imagine her surprise when she walked into the office on her first day to find that she was Calista's boss and earning four times her wage.

In the world today, a high school education may help you get a job, but it will not start you on the road to a good career. A college education will help your career if you choose a good major and work to make good marks.

The good jobs are reserved for those who graduate college because those people have learned how to learn. Training them is easier. The best jobs are reserved for those who pursue a graduate degree with a broader scope of knowledge, They don't have to be trained and they have proven they are willing to go the extra mile for their profession.

No matter what your age or situation, a path to finish school is always available if you really want to do it.

Meditation: *Please help me to learn every day even if it's just by reading on my own. I will use my knowledge to improve my life and the lives of others.*

__Body:__

While sitting, rotate your shoulders in wide then small circles then wide again at least twenty times. This is a stress buster and will do great things for your chest as well!

Keeping your shoulder muscles in shape prevents common injuries and improving flexibility.

When you increase your reach, you make it possible to do things you might not have been able to do before; like climb, improve your golf swing and get to items on taller shelves.

__Money:__

Check out and apply for scholarships. You will be surprised at how many you are eligible for! Also check with your employer and organizations to which you belong. Some scholarships go un-awarded each year because no one knows about them!

__Mind:__

If you are still alive there is no reason not to finish a degree *if you want one*. It is expensive but there are loans, scholarships and grants available with research. You can take courses online, at night or on weekends. A degree gives you more credibility *and* more confidence.

Joke:
New report: Use of elevators is on the rise.

Day #19

Stand Up for Your Beliefs

I was sitting with my retired mother in a casino dining room when I heard a man beside me at a full table telling a racist joke. Some at his table looked around nervously before laughing. I tried to smile but only managed a grimace. My mother poked me in the ribs. He told another awful "joke" and I looked around for another place to sit. There were none.

Suddenly something I had heard that morning popped into my head. I waited for him to finish his joke and then spoke up.

"I've got one. A duck walks into a 7-11 and says "Give me some Chapstick, and put it on my bill!" The clerk just looks at him because ducks don't speak English. The duck tries again but can't get through to the clerk. The duck finally walks out, frustrated, wondering why he'd need Chapstick anyway, since he has no lips."

There was a moment of silence then someone booed and the whole table started to laugh. Maybe it was a relief that it didn't turn out to be a racist joke or because the boo was funny. It set off a series of *funny* duck jokes. No one felt obligated to laugh and everyone felt compelled to boo the bad ones!

Faced with a situation where you feel obliged to stand up for your beliefs, try to find a non-confrontational way. You will never change a bigoted mind by preaching, but people will follow a good example.

Meditation: *Please give me strength to stand up for what I feel is right in a way that will guide my adversary and not threaten him. I will lead by example.*

Body:

While sitting raise your feet to knee level and rotate your ankles in circles for a count of twenty. This helps blood flow to your legs and tightens calf muscles.

You can tighten the muscles inside your thighs by moving your legs apart and together while doing this exercise as well.

Money:

When a cashier asks you if you want to donate a dollar to charity, say no but put the dollar aside to donate anyway. Corporations earn interest on your money then get a tax break at the end of the year! YOU choose the charity. You get the tax break!

Mind:

Do you laugh at racist or sexist jokes?
Do you tell them?
To increase your integrity among your peers, learn jokes that won't make ANYONE feel bad, and refuse to laugh at jokes that belittle other people.

For today's joke, read today's story lesson,
it's an important one.

Day #20

"Do" to Teach

My daughter and her friends were walking in the park one winter afternoon when they heard music. They followed the sound to a woman playing a violin.
In the cold, the resin on her bow was hardening and the sound that came out of her instrument was a bit sharp. Two of the girls wanted to walk on, but one of them noticed that there were only a few quarters in the woman's case, probably the ones she had put there to get people started. She grabbed my daughter and spun her around. Soon they were kicking and reeling to the music. The other two girls joined in and they made up a crazy, funny dance to the now more cheerful music.

It didn't take long for people to show up to watch and clap along with the girls as they whirled and leaped, getting more coordinated all the time.
When the song ended nearly everyone dropped a dollar or two into the empty case. The woman looked at the 10-year-olds with such gratitude as I have never seen before and I couldn't keep tears out of my eyes. A moment passed between them, a mutual "thank you" and then the girls ran off to do something else.

Each time my daughter sees a street musician she donates, I don't think she remembers why. Sometimes she dances, once she even pulled me into it!
I am grateful for the lesson that little girl (Chloe) taught us about seizing the moment for generosity. That gift is a beautiful memory!

Meditation: *Please help me to see good and build on it in an unlikely moment and to enjoy the music of life. I will lead by example and teach others to appreciate life's little gifts.*

Body:

While standing facing a wall, point your toe and stretch your leg out as far up behind you as you can comfortably. Relax and repeat on both legs at least ten times. This is great for your thighs and butt, and you will notice as you progress, you can go higher!

Money:

If you don't have extra money to donate, give TIME! Outside of making you feel great, volunteering can help you network with other responsible volunteers.

Mind:

Learn a small musical instrument like an ocarina ukulele or harmonica. Practicing and making up new songs is great for your memory and your mood!

Joke:
When you aren't making cents, find a new job.

Day #21

Be Succinct

Does this sound familiar?

"Hand me that thing please."
"This thing?"
"No, that one beside it."
"This thing?"
"No, the other side of it. "
This?
"No, back. That."
"Ohhh, *this* thing!"
"Yes, that."

Wouldn't it have been simpler to say, "Hand me that red Phillips head screwdriver?"

So often we think we are saving time by being short and we expect people to read our minds. How many arguments have you been involved in where you expected the other person to know what you were talking about when you said "Remember that time…?"

If it seems as though the other sex speaks a different language, you're not wrong, they do.
Women use hand gestures and facial signals and men use technical words and short directives.
Children cannot follow multi-step directions until they are 10 to 12 years old. (Some adults *never* understand verbal multi-step directions.)

Whenever possible strive to be succinct. "Please, hand me that chocolate caa… I mean red apple on top."

Meditation: *Please help me to remember that not everyone thinks exactly as I do. Help me to be clear and easily understood. I will strive to speak clearly and give more information when I am communicating with someone who may not understand me.*

Body:

Three weeks! Weigh yourself. Measure your neck, chest, arms, waist, legs and hips. Take pictures, blog and/or update the chart!

At this point people are probably starting to say things like, "Did you get a new haircut?" (If you're following the plan you did, but that's not it.) "Is that a new shirt?" or "You look great today." They might not know you are losing weight and tightening up but *you* do and you're starting to see the results. Keep up the good work!

Money:

Little things can save you a lot of money. Packing his lunch for one year saved a friend $840. (He spent $4 a day on lunch.) Cut out the morning cappuccino to save another $840! What could you do with $1,680?

Mind:

Practice expressing yourself more succinctly. Think of precise ways to get your point across to save time and be better understood.

Joke:
Jet lag is a "terminal" illness.

Day #22

Use the Knowledge of Others (Quote Eloquence)

Using quotations is a quick way to draw upon the wisdom of elders you have never met.

By memorizing just a few good quotations you can add wit and wisdom to any conversation. For general purposes it is important to memorize quotes on stupidity, arrogance, religion, love, and youth, but be careful.

"...one of the best ways to get yourself a reputation as a dangerous citizen these days is to go about repeating the very phrases which our founding fathers used in the struggle for independence." *-Charles Austin Beard*

Also, before you quote someone, especially in writing, be sure you know from whom the quote came.
A quote widely attributed to basketball star Shaquille O'Neal, "Excellence is not a singular act, but a habit. You are what you repeatedly do.", was actually a paraphrase of a quote by Aristotle. This has been happening for centuries as noticed by Sir Winston Churchill who said:

"I am reminded of the professor who, in his declining hours, was asked by his devoted pupils for his final counsel. He replied, 'Verify your quotations.'"

Use quotations sparingly, credit their originator, interject them well and people will listen, after all, who among us is qualified to argue with Socrates who said

"The only true wisdom is in knowing that you know nothing."

Meditation: *Please help me to draw on the wisdom of men and women who are wiser than I. I will be humble enough to call on the time-honored words of wiser ancestors to clarify my viewpoints.*

Body:

Lie on your back and with your arms to your side raise first one leg then the other slowly straight up to the ceiling and back down. Repeat ten to twenty times.

This is great for your tummy, thighs and even your butt. It doesn't take a lot of time, you can do it before you get out of bed in the morning or when you are going to sleep at night. Add it to your daily repertoire if you want to see better results.

Money:

"Money never made a man happy yet, nor will it. The more a man has, the more he wants. Instead of filling a vacuum, it makes one." Benjamin Franklin.

Mind:

Continuous effort - not strength or intelligence - is the key to unlocking our potential"
Winston Churchill

Joke:
""I won't stand for that!" – Achilles"

Day #23

Be Grateful for Flaws

In 1980 everyone had straight or "feathered" hair, even girls born with curly hair, because they would get up early to iron and spray it until it was hard as a helmet.

That is before Steven Leeds moved to town. He was strikingly handsome and he never seemed interested in any of the starry-eyed girls who followed him around. One day there was an electrical storm that cut power in the neighborhood where Steven and my friend Cherise lived.

Cherise had bushy, red, curly hair. I was one of only a few who knew that because, like everyone, she ironed it every day.

That day, she unconvincingly tried to convince her mother that she was sick but, in the end, she walked to the bus stop in the rain, her hair swirling angrily in the wild wind. As she plopped onto the bench on front of her best friend she said, "Braid this quick before anyone sees it!"

Steven, who had for once been unnoticed, spoke up. "I think it looks pretty as it is." Her friend reached for a strand. Cherise gave her a tap and a look that said, "Touch one hair and you will die!"

Word spread fast and by the end of the week there were many more curly-haired girls at our school. "Big hair" then seemed to happen overnight.

Steven's family moved away a few weeks later but I never saw Cherise's hair straight again.

That one comment on a *perceived flaw* made it the biggest fashion sensation to ever hit my school.

Meditation: *Please help me to understand that what I see as a defect may be a gift in disguise. Help me to embrace my difference and accept differences in others.*

Body:

While sitting, hold your arms straight out to your sides, keeping your arms straight slowly bring your hands together and press them against one another. Repeat ten to twenty times. This is a great chest developer!

Breast size means nothing. If you look at modern culture you will see that women of all sizes enjoy great popularity these day. (Chest size for men as well.) The trick is confidence. When you project your satisfaction with your natural body people respond by liking it too. Hold your head up and walk with posture and pride. You are wonderful.

Money:

"Flawed" appliances often go on sale for a fraction of their price. A new refrigerator that sells for $2000 can go for $800 if there is a dent in it. A new front panel is $60. Do a bit of research and save a fortune!

Mind:

Ancient Chinese artists always included a deliberate flaw in their work. Human creation is never perfect. Accept that your flaws make you unique and use them to your advantage.

Joke:
A missing letter can make a word of difference.

Day #24

Be Focused

When searching the sky for constellations, we find a few key stars to confirm our position. It's impossible to do through thick clouds.

When your mind is clouded by a lot of distractions it is easy to get confused and mistake one priority for another unless you remember which direction you are facing! Concentrate on your main goal like a guiding star at least once a day and look for ways to direct your efforts toward that goal.

You may have to wash your car, pick up your dry cleaning, shop for a birthday gift and try that new Thai restaurant, but if it is your wife's birthday, you had better not forget the gift or you may find yourself sleeping in a clean car covered by newly pressed shirts and reeking of the Mu Dang she threw at you.

Focusing on the most important star frees your mind of all the other stars to let you see the constellation. Once you have accomplished the top priority you can concentrate on the next until the whole list is complete.

Making a list helps, but once you establish the habit of setting and then focusing to complete important goals it will become automatic.

Meditation: *Please help me to clear my mind of thoughts and feelings that do not get me closer to my goal. Help me to concentrate first on things that matter. I will set priorities and work on things that are most important first.*

Body:

While sitting, alternate raising your ankles up to the height of your knees as if you are splashing water while sitting on the side of a pool. If you have access to a pool do this exercise there.

Repeat at least twenty times to tighten those saggy knees. By now some of the fat should be gone, leaving them slightly looser! This exercise will help bind the connective tissue and tighten up the potential sag as you continue to lose unhealthy fat.

Money:

Focus on paying off debts with the highest balance-to-interest ratio first. If you can, consolidate your payments to one loan with a low rate. Credit unions often offer good rates on consolidation loans.

Mind:

It's easier to focus on a task if you set a definite action and a deadline to follow through.

Rather than thinking, "My car is dirty." say out loud, "I will wash my car by 1:00." and it's more likely to be true.

Joke:
Two fortune tellers meet on the street.
The first says, "You're fine, how am I?"

Day #25

Try Something New

I tried water skiing under the tutelage of some bad teachers. I broke several blood vessels in my arms getting up on the skis the first time. Later that day I tried a second time and a large fish jumped out of the water in front of me, leaving a scar that I still have. To add insult to injury I fell on my face getting in the boat causing a bloody nose. It was a miserable day.

I hated water skiing and boating so much that it kept me out of the water for ten years.
One weekend a friend with a boat tricked me into going "fishing". (I intended get even with Scarfish's offspring!)

When we were far from shore he said I'd love power tubing. (Essentially water skiing on your butt.) I protested. No matter how fun it sounded, I would not do it. I finally agreed to try it but went last, hoping that everyone would be tired and I would get out of it. Finally, not wanting to be a drag ☺ I gave it a shot.

Thirty seconds into the experience, as I skipped over the waves, I uttered an involuntary "Who hoo!" then I promptly flipped headfirst into the water! I checked myself for injuries and finding none, climbed back onto the tube to feel that exhilaration again. I've decided that it is my new favorite weekend activity.

I missed so many boating trips over the years because of one bad experience. The tubing adventure taught me a very valuable lesson: Just because something reminds you of a bad experience, doesn't mean you shouldn't try it.

Meditation: *Please help me to keep my mind open to new experiences. I will try something new this week with no expectations.*

Body:

On your hands and knees lift one leg up to the height of your bottom (no further) then slowly lower it and repeat ten times per leg. This is an excellent butt buster!

You may need to place a pillow or a couch cushion under your knees to protect them if you haven't been on your knees for many years.

As you lose weight and there is less pressure on them you can do this exercise on a yoga mat or even the floor, but for now protect those knees you are working so hard to make strong.

Money:

Try a pay per month cell phone service for a few months and save a lot of money. They often use the exact same service you're using now so you can keep your phone and there is no expensive contract.

Mind:

Try something you think you can't do in a new way. Search online for math tricks, tell a story to a kid, or paint an "abstract" with your non-dominate hand!

Joke:
If you can't be positive, just be double negative!

Day #26

Ask for Advice

Jerry called his brother Alan and told him he thought his wife was having an affair.

"I'm on my way to an attorney's office. He works with a private investigator. He says he can find out who she's going out with."

"Jerry, I think you are jumping the gun, man. What makes you think she is sleeping around?"

"She hangs up the phone when I walk in the room. She's been doing a lot of "errands", and she won't tell me where she went yesterday afternoon. I know she left, her car was warm when I borrowed it."

Jerry broke down. He told Alan that he loved his wife, thought she loved him too and had not seen it coming.

Alan told him to sleep on hiring an attorney, to give his wife the benefit of the doubt and see if he could open the lines of communication first. He said "I'll come get you; we will take a drive to get your mind off the situation."

Alan picked Jerry up and drove him to their parent's house where his wife was waiting, along with thirty of his best friends to surprise him for his birthday, which he had completely forgotten was the next day.

Jerry did a wise thing. He called his brother for advice.

Sometimes when we are faced with a crisis situation we are tempted to go it alone out of embarrassment or to avoid burdening friends. Sometimes a little help from someone you truly trust is all it takes to divert the crisis and get things back to normal.

Meditation: *Please help me to be humble enough to ask for advice when things get overwhelming. I understand that an outsider might have knowledge that I don't and may be able to help.*

Body:
While sitting on the floor with your legs together in front of you, come as close as you can to touching your toes. Don't overdo it, only stretch as far as you can comfortably stretch.
Raise your arms toward the ceiling and try again. Your flexibility will increase a bit each time and increase by leaps and bounds once your belly fat is gone and your tendons and muscles are used to being stretched.

Mind:
If you have a problem with someone, ask them to explain themselves. We tend to read people according to *our* moods, sometimes we are wrong!

Joke:
I lost my mood ring... not sure how I feel about this.

Money:
If you have a good payment history, ask your credit card companies for a lower rate. If they won't lower it, look for a better card!

Day #27

Consider the Source of Advice

Alice thought her husband was cheating on her. She called her new friend Gina who had been hanging around a lot more lately and asked her what to do.

Gina said, "Leave him."
Alice did.
Gina moved in with Alice's husband a week later.

Alice lost a friend and a bad husband but learned a lesson about advice: Consider the source.
Had Alice take a moment to think before calling Gina she would have recognized that Gina had been around more often *talking to her husband*. She even called a few times for help with a car problem when she knew Alice wouldn't be able to come along. (Alice's husband had also been too excited about helping.)

There are professionals; clergymen, counselors, group meetings, even trusted family members with whom you could speak before you ask advice of someone who might not have your best interests at heart.

You wouldn't ask a pickpocket to hold your wallet; you shouldn't ask someone who may want your spouse to help you with your relationship.

Meditation: *Please help me to look for a proper source for advice when facing a difficult time. I will consider recent behavior when deciding who has my best interests at heart.*

Body:

Stand with your legs apart and bend at your waist. Place your hands on the floor and walk yourself down until you are lying on your belly, then walk yourself back up.

If you feel an unnatural pull or if anything hurts, stop. We are trying to strengthen and lengthen our bodies and that takes time.

This stretches your calves and back and strengthens your arms and abs. It's difficult if you've never done it so don't stress yourself. Do it against a wall.

Money:

Shop around, talk to a few advisors before choosing an investment firm. Treat your money like a child; leave it with someone you trust!

Mind:

Seek the advice of a trusted clergyman, counselor or psychologist, and check credentials when you are dealing with depression, addiction, or family issues! Your mind is complex and the way you think affects not just you, but people who love you. Choose someone with sufficient training AND experience.

Joke:
A lady told me that I had cute knuckles, but I know that it was just a backhanded compliment.

Day #28

Don't Always Follow Advice

My mother was making dinner while talking to my aunt Clara on the phone and keeping an eye on my four-year-old brother when I asked her if I should wear the white pants or the blue jeans. I held them in front of her. She glanced up and pointed at the white pants. I favored the jeans but I ran to my room and put them on. I was running late to a friend's party.

I threw on a sweater and dashed out the front door, down the gravel driveway and across the field to my friend's house. I smoothed my hair and walked confidently into the room where all eyes shifted down to my pant legs that were *spattered muddy brown* from the wet dirt road. Jeans would have hidden the mess.

I ducked back out, ran home and scowled at my overworked mother on my way to change into the jeans I should have worn in the first place. I knew it had been raining but my mother had been inside all day. If I had trusted myself and worn the jeans I would not have missed out on the first twenty minutes of the party which I returned to with far less confidence.

Even if someone has your best interests at heart there are times when it is wise not to follow the advice. Trust yourself first.

However, whatever you decide, you must take responsibility for it!

Meditation: *Please help me to trust myself first in matters in which I have asked for help. I will remember that advice is only as good as the knowledge of the giver.*

Body:

Four weeks! Weigh yourself. Measure your neck, chest, arms, waist, legs and hips. Take pictures, blog and/or update the chart! You should see some real results now!

If you've made it through the month, you deserve a treat but don't use food as a reward.
Dance or play pool with friends, get your nails done, buy a new ball cap, or do something to keep yourself on the right path.

Last winter was 90 days long and you probably can't remember most of it. 90 days will fly by.

Money:

Ask your insurance agent if you qualify for any discounts or raise your deductible and invest the savings for if you ever need it! All money you save (and make) over that deductible amount is profit!

Mind:

Practice affirmations. They are not silly if properly used. Believe that you are wise. Say it out loud. Smile when you look in the mirror, wink if it makes you laugh! Be nice to yourself! Have fun!

Joke:
People who are gluten free get a lot of hate, but I really respect them for going against the grain.

Day #29

Don't Insert Yourself

Tara had a feeling her son, Eric, might be gay but his father was always trying to find the perfect girl for him. Whenever they met for dinner her husband nudged him and winked whenever he saw an attractive girl.
Tara noticed Eric's nervous laugh and felt it was her duty to intervene in the situation.

She invited him to lunch and told him she knew he was gay and recommended he tell his father. Eric was aghast, not that his mother thought he was gay, but that she was crossing such a personal line. He told her that he wasn't gay but *was* disturbed that she thought his personal life was her business.
She refused to back off, emailing him articles on coming out and even stopping by his apartment unannounced in the early morning to see for herself.
He cut off all communication with her.

One evening they all bumped into each other at a restaurant where Eric introduced them to his wife. They had been dating for a year. He didn't bring her home because his father was against interracial dating. Surprisingly, his father was instantly taken with the girl and there were no problems between the two of them.

It took months for Eric to come to terms with Tara's intrusion. Eventually they made peace but they lost a lot of time trying to fix the trust that her interference had broken.

Meditation: *Please help me to be still when matters don't require my intervention. I will give advice when asked and when someone is in danger but will keep my counsel until it is required.*

Body:

Try to walk another half a mile today but pay attention to your body for signs of strain or fatigue. You are eating less now and you may not have the energy to push yourself.

You may be more aware because you are now paying attention to your body. It will tell you when to slow down and when you can push it a little farther. You are doing this to improve your whole life, and it's working!

Money:

Repair things as they break to save money on bigger expenses. A leaky transmission hose can be fixed for $50, a transmission, run on no fluid, will break and can cost a fortune to fix!

Mind:

Read about others from their perspective. If you are young, read AARP's website. If you are straight, read an LBGTQ website that you wouldn't ordinarily read. Google translate a foreign news site to see that most people that you believe are not like you, really are in many ways.

Joke:
When a fruit truck spills over, it creates a traffic jam.

Day #30

Recognize Your Passions

Maybe you've been looking for the thing that will make you happy *and* make you money but can't zero in on the one thing that you want to do.

One method of finding your passion is to picture yourself living your ideal work day. What time do you wake up afternoon, morning, evening? You wake up shower and brush your teeth… now what?

Do you find yourself in an office with people who have a sense of humor? Are you the boss or an employee? Are you outdoors or indoors? Gardening, filing papers, or making sales calls? Are you alone or with others?

Pre-living your ideal work day will help you sort through what's important to you.

Denise was a mother of two who had gone back to work in a manufacturing plant after ten years at home. The noise and smell gave her a headache, her schedule changed every week, and she longed for the quiet afternoons she spent sewing or reading at home but she couldn't afford to give up her job.
She went to the library to browse classified ads on her day off and, on a whim, applied to the library for a job.

A week later she was shelving books and helping patrons find books and DVDs. The rate of pay is the same and she loves her job!

By recognizing that she loves quiet afternoons she was able to find a job that is making her happy!

Meditation: *Please help me to try to search my mind for things that I value to figure out where I belong in the world. I will write out the elements of my ideal day and study them for clues to my ideal job.*

Body:

While sitting, breathe in for ten seconds and out for ten seconds whenever you think of it.

This should always be part of your daily WISDOM, but we can forget how important it is. Deep breathing increases your metabolism as it feeds oxygen to your cells.

You may find deep breathing boosts your energy like a cup of coffee. Unlike coffee you can have it anytime you want, it costs nothing, and you never have a caffeine crash.

Money:

If you find a cute little thing, take a photo of it for your bulletin board, don't buy it. Spending just $20 a week on knick-knacks for your home, wardrobe or hair, adds up to $1,040 a year. That's as much as a ticket to Europe!

Mind:

To help curb your spending, think of your higher savings goal. Are you saving for a new car? Imagine yourself cruising the wind blowing through your hair.
Saving for a trip? Imagine yourself on the beach, skiing, or taking photos in your destination.

Joke:
I made my bed every day for a week. Honestly, it seems like a waste of lumber.

Day #31

Maintain Control of Your Passions

Jay loved fixing things up. He remodeled his apartment and the owner was so impressed he raised the rent.

Jay was furious and decided he wanted to be the landlord. He put his life savings down on a house to renovate it for resale. As he worked on it he decided that he liked carpentry enough to do it for a living.

He quit his job and had business cards made to give to anyone who might require his services as a contractor. Within two months, costly repairs on the dilapidated house he bought forced him to sell his truck to make payments. The work he thought would come rolling in went to trained licensed contractors.
Jay lost the house he had worked so hard to repair and what was left of his bank account. His back-up car broke down and he had no money to replace it.
He rented a mobile home (refused to do repairs) and worked at a restaurant, the only job he could find within walking distance.

The moral of Jay's story is, don't jump in head first until you test the depth of the water.

Stay tuned. Jay's story has a happy ending.

Meditation: *Please help me to take my time choosing a path that may affect my family or change my life in an unpleasant way. I will maintain my passions by looking for opportunities to do them on a temporary basis first.*

Body:

Do squats while you wash your hands before meals and after going to the bathroom. No one can see you, you have the sink to hold onto if you fall off balance and it will give you a little boost before you return to work, food or whatever you were doing.

If you try to do it every time you wash your hands it will become as much a habit as drying your hands. (During which you can do squats too!)

Don't worry if it's a public bathroom, anyone who sees you might pick up the habit too. Good deed for the day!

Money:

If you have been depositing your change, coffee and take-out lunch money you may have enough to invest in a mutual fund. There are some funds that will allow you to invest as little as $100. *Find a one that matches your own interests for best results.*

Mind:

Take your time making important decisions. Anything worth having is worth waiting for and being impulsive seldom pays. Weigh pros and cons on paper if necessary.

Joke:
What do you get when you cross-breed a bear and a cow?
I have no idea but I wouldn't try milking it.

Day #32

Use Your Passions

After yesterday's tale, you may be thinking "What good is discovering my passion if it will lead me to ruin?" The answer is, if you channel your passions, you can profit!

Jay had a rare weekend off so a neighbor asked him to help build a deck on his mobile home and offered an old pick-up truck as payment.

Jay built a sturdy decorative deck in only two days including clean-up. It impressed the neighbor so much he gave him a hundred dollars as well as the truck. Jay used the money to fix the truck and sold his car.

After seeing the deck, other neighbors hired him to build decks for them. He set a fair price and built each one quickly with great attention to detail. His decks improved the quality of life for residents of the park who then began to take pride in their homes. Jay was hired to do a lot of improvements and started building a reputation as a hardworking man of his word. It wasn't long until he was back on his feet and out of debt.

He advertised his services at mobile home parks he passed, and soon he developed a beautiful portfolio. Jay now makes a good living building decks and doing repairs to mobile homes.

He says what he likes most is seeing the smile of satisfaction when an elderly lady walks onto her porch for the first time. (His second favorite thing is the cookies they often bake for him!)

Meditation: *Please help me to use my passion in a way that benefits others. I realize that by doing my best with things that make me happy I will profit as well and will build a happier life.*

Body:

Today do something that doesn't feel like exercise. Play catch with a child or fetch with your dog. Take a window shopping tour of the local mall. (Don't go to the food court!) Get used to moving more in what you already do and make life your exercise.

Money:

A good way to keep the good graces of friends who loan you equipment is to return it in better shape than when you borrowed it. Clean tools, machines full of fuel, and prompt returns will make you a welcome borrower and save you money.

Mind:

Sometimes a talent one takes for granted can be a marketable talent. Remember the whistle from Otis Redding's Dock of the Bay? It was added to conceal the fact that a last verse had not been written; it made the song a number-one hit.

Joke:
I got a photo from a speeding camera through the mail. I sent it back – way too expensive and really bad quality.

Day #33

Don't Let Others Think for You

"If your friends jumped off a bridge would you jump too?" sounded silly when your mom said it, but how many times did you get drunk at a party because you thought your friends would think less of you if you didn't? Or how many times have you bought something just because your friends would think was cool?

Often, we forget we have the opportunity to lead and don't have the obligation to follow.

My son is diabetic and can't drink alcohol. At a party a friend said she was relieved to find him. She had been afraid to say no to the drinks that were put in her hand and when she heard him say, "No thanks, I'm good." She had the nerve to say it too. It didn't make her look un-cool. In fact, when she drove her idiot friends home later, they were all grateful for her moderation!

In a groups we can get talked into doing things we know are wrong just to keep from standing out.

In 15 minutes at a mall food court, I counted 47 girls all wearing jeans, a t-shirt over a tank top, and white tennis shoes. It was almost a uniform!

I overheard a girl at another table say to her friend "I think you are the only one I know who doesn't have a Hollister shirt." The other girl said "I'm too lit to wear what everyone else is wearing." I wanted to hug her!

A plasma TV won't make you cool. Knowledge from the documentary you saw on your old computer might!

Wearing a brand name pair of shoes won't make you cool. Creaming opponents at basketball probably will.

Who will remember your shirt, your television, or your shoes in ten years? But your chill, your smarts, and your 3-point shots could become legendary.

Meditation: *Please help me realize that I don't have to own popular things to be accepted. I will use what I have to its full potential and better **myself** so that I shine*

Body:

You may find your clothes are outgrowing you. Take your favorites in for tailoring. Sell your old ones.

Wearing clothes that fit is important to your self-esteem and it's safer. If your pants fall down when you are running to catch the bus, the humiliation will be nothing compared to the pain!

Styles change, but not much. Notice what people wear and look for those things among your "skinny clothes".

Money:

When shopping with friends resist the urge to buy because they are buying. You can have a good time helping them choose without killing your bank account!

Mind:

How did your favorite toy feel, smell, look? Drawing on memories of long forgotten items can strengthen your memory and give you a happy uplift!

Joke:
Why did the dinosaur cross the road?
Because the chicken hadn't evolved yet.

Day #34

Don't Think for Others

Tomi's younger brother and her sweetie had talked marriage for two years and said they were still unwed. They claimed it was because they were daunted by the difficulty of making wedding arrangements.

She jumped at thechance to help and arranged a surprise moonlight ceremony on a boat on Lake Erie with a reception to follow in the dining cabin.

She invited both families, and as the date approached and excitement built, Tomi asked sneaky questions to get more ideas for the big day. Boy was she surprised when he found out her brother's girlfriend hated boats and was especially susceptible to seasickness! Even more so when she found out her brother didn't want to get married at all and was unhappy in their relationship! They broke up a few months later.

She lost a thousand dollars and learned a valuable lesson: It never pays to think for someone else.

Meditation: *Please help me to understand that although my friends' choices may not be my own they are entitled to them. I will make an effort to understand and accept their actions without assuming that my way is the best way.*

Body:

Stretch everything each morning before you get out of bed to get blood flowing and for a good reason to stay in bed a few minutes longer!

Stretching prepares muscles for exertion and helps reduce injuries. It also tells your mind to prepare for what lies beyond your bedroom door.

Mind:

Delegate responsibilities to take a load off of your mind and help others feel more responsible. If you have a hundred errands and someone owes you a favor, allow them to repay it by doing errands for you!

Money:

When choosing gifts for someone else don't let price be the only guide. Sometimes framing a photo can be a much better gift than a gadget that will end up in a tag sale next summer!

Joke:
I always do my gardening when my wife is singing. Just to prove to the neighbors there's no domestic abuse!

Day #35

Don't Be Too Sympathetic

Brownie was the sweetest dog that ever lived and it was heartbreaking when she broke her right rear leg.

She was rushed to a vet and the leg was set. Soon she was healed and running again. However, months passed and she still held up the leg when she ran. Two more visits to the vet and hundreds of dollars later, no one could explain what was wrong. Then the vet had a great idea. He bandaged Brownie's *other* rear leg forcing her to use the right one when she ran.

She ran flawlessly on the "sore" leg. One week later the fake bandaged was removed from her left leg and to everyone's amusement she held up the uninjured leg when running as if it was broken!

Sometimes we hold up our own phantom injuries.

An unhappy childhood can be an excuse for failure. Ironically, surviving trauma gives us more ammunition in the battle for success! We have training from already having overcome a huge obstacle!

The best therapy for someone who thrives on sympathy is to give them a replacement for the misery. Instead of saying, "You poor dear." say, "Wow, you are such a fighter!" Some sympathy is warranted but instead of making excuses for someone who slacks in the name of personal history give them a reason to rise above it!

Meditation: *Please give me the kindness to be sympathetic when it is necessary and the wisdom and strength to be encouraging instead of sympathetic when the situation calls for it.*

__Body:__

Five weeks! Weigh yourself. Measure your neck, chest, arms, waist, legs and hips. Take pictures, blog and/or update the chart!

You will probably find your body is a little more flexible at this point. You can reach lower and higher than you could before. Stretching on a regular basis is important for a body, all mammals do it. (Just watch a dog or cat wake from a nap.)
Yoga is based on a series of stretches. You've been doing living-yoga for five weeks now!

__Mind:__

Think of how others want you to treat them. Would you be the same in their shoes? What differences can you find between the way you treat people and the way you would want to be treated?

__Money:__

Some people collect things to make up for being poor as a child. Some buy expensive items to make up for low self-esteem. Explore the reason for overspending and you might end up saving a fortune!

Joke:
Light travels faster than sound. That is why some people appear quite bright – until you hear them talk.

Day #36
Don't Play on Sympathy

A woman in my town bakes pies for members of the church who have been ill. One man in the congregation raved about her peach pie at a bake sale and a week later came down with a horrible migraine that kept him from attending services. A fresh pie helped him recover.

A few months later he sprained his ankle and missed another service but was considerate enough to write a note to the pastor with his pained regrets. An apple pie made him feel better.

That autumn he had a feverish bout of the flu and sent a friend with news of his illness. Apparently, he was unfamiliar with the phrase "Feed a cold, starve a fever." No pie arrived, pastor's orders.

The following Sunday he came to church with a frown on his face. After the service, at a rummage sale, he mumbled about being forgotten in his time of need. The pastor, a man with a sense of humor remarked, 'You're either going to have to come up with a lifelong illness or break down and *buy* some pies!

He did, and he's been healthy most Sunday since!

It doesn't take long for someone to spot a sympathy ploy and it is a rare person who will play along.

Milking sympathy is dangerous. In times of honest pain there is nothing like a helping hand or a kind word to set a person back on his feet but in cases where sympathy is used to manipulate it can backfire!

Meditation: *Please help me to be self-reliant unless I actually need help. Then please grant me the humility to ask for help. I will be aware of times in which I am using the sympathy of others as a crutch to keep me from moving forward.*

Body:

Standing with your arms to your sides and your fingers and thumbs out, slowly reach straight up as high as you can, then reach higher. Lower your arms to your sides and without bending your waist, reach as low as you can. Repeat 10 times. This is great for shoulder flexibility and for your spine. Note how your back felt when you reached higher the second time.

Breath in while reaching up and out while reaching down. You can do this exercise while seated or while bending at a 90-degree angle. (to include your core in the stretch) It's energizing!

Money:

Days missed from work don't only cost your company money, they will put you behind in your work. That might result in your being overlooked for a raise.

Mind:

People who are told there is a cold going around are twice as likely to come down with symptoms. If you feel headachy and sore ask yourself, "Is this really happening or is this stress and exhaustion?"

Joke:
Nothing reminds us of how often we usually fart like a 12-hour date.

Day #37

Change with the Seasons

Most people have summer clothes; light weather fabrics that help the body adjust to the temperature.

Human beings have summer feelings as well; different behaviors that match the seasons.

Spring is a season of renewal. People find themselves attracted to the opposite sex and restless. Bright lights bring out optimism lacking in winter days when the sun only appears for 8 hours at a time.

Summer is a time for relaxation and procrastination as people vacation and lounge, conserving energy in the sun or stay indoors where it is air conditioned and cool. Many people separate themselves from their usual groups and learn more about new friendships.

Autumn brings people outdoors and together again. There are more parties in the autumn than any other season as people strengthen bonds and bring new people back to their established circles.

As days start to get shorter and colder again, people "hibernate" by reading and watching television. Tempers run high as people are in closed spaces together and their bodies crave sunshine and fresh air.

Understanding human instinct is a step toward understanding the motivations of friends and loved ones as seasons change. Knowing why you are more apt to snap at your loved ones in the cold of winter may make it easier for you to resist the temptation to do so. We must remember that we're not the only ones feeling the change of seasons to cope with those changes.

Meditation: *Please help me to remember that human beings are animals and are susceptible to changes of seasons just like penguins and rabbits. Our habits are natural and have an underlying purpose. I will act in a loving manner anticipating the next change of seasons.*

Body:

While sitting, stretch your upper body as far to the right and then the left as comfortably possible. It's great for your waist and back.

Be careful not to stretch too far or too fast. Only go as far as is comfortable. The human spine is a complicated thing and can be injured due to unexpected torsion or exertion.

Money:

Wash your clothes and put them in plastic box with a paper towel sachet filled with baking soda and closed with a rubber band. When you get them out the following season they will still smell good and be ready to wear!

Mind:

Keep a "sunlight bulb" in a lamp close to where you work in the winter to beat the wintertime blues. There are certain colors in a sunlight bulb that satisfy a need for sunlight that we miss during cold weather.

Joke:
Sometimes I feel like a God. People totally forget that I exist and only approach me when they need something.

Day #38

Read the News

Have you ever been in the room with a group of people discussing something you don't understand when one of them turns to you and says something like, "What do you think of the situation in Myanmar?"

On occasion you can get out of answering using tricks like "I love them with a glass of milk, wink, nudge. Or "I'm withholding judgment until I know more, what is your take on the issue?" but some will see through that and know you were caught unaware.

The ONLY way to stay abreast of important issues is to read the news. A quick browse of headlines and a few lines of an article is often all it takes to get the general idea about something. A thorough reading will help you grasp the nuances and be able to converse in any group. For the best take, it is important to read newspapers from other cities and countries; they can be found in any library or can often be viewed online.

An alternative to reading the news would be to listen to and watch several radio and television stations. It is hard to get the whole story from one outlet.

Knowing what's going on in the world will not only help your dinner party conversations it will enable you to meet and converse with people from different backgrounds in a work or social environment. It will help you vote with more clarity and will help solidify your viewpoint on important issues.

Meditation: *Please help me to stay informed about events that are happening in my world to keep me from becoming closed-minded and dull. I will use information from news sources to strengthen my relationships with people in my social and networking circles.*

Body:

While sitting rotate your shoulders in wide then small circles then wide again at least twenty times. Let your arms hang loosely at your sides and relax your neck. This is a stress buster and flexibility builder that may even relieve a headache.

Money:

If you prefer a paper newspaper and wish to save money visit the library or ask your favorite waitress to save today's copy for you to read at lunch. Someone always leaves one on a breakfast table.

Mind:

Do the crossword puzzle! It expands your vocabulary and teaches little-known facts!

Joke:
It's not such a fine restaurant when you ask a waiter for a toothpick and he says, "I'm sorry but you'll have to wait, they are currently all in use."

Day #39

Don't Take the Media at Face Value

The importance of being informed comes with one caveat: Know the source of your information.

Some news outlets will insist that they are fair and balanced, but a quick comparison with a few other outlets will make it clear that they are conveying only one side of all issues.

Everyone has an opinion. Opinions can be swayed by information. There is no way to form an educated opinion about any topic if you only hear one side of it.

I attended a lecture at a college on the threat of organized religion. The following evening, I attended a lecture in a church on the threat of biased education.

I heard a lot of the same ideas in both lectures used *against* the logic of the other. In newspapers and on television stations the same is true. The same talking points are used by several news outlets to illustrate the opposite point of view.

Recognize that some media is owned by members of one political party and some are owned by another. You may get great information, but in both cases, you will learn what that that corporation wants you to know.

An informed citizen looks at several sides of any story by visiting websites and stations that report news from different points of view.

Meditation: *Please help me to understand that media is owned by people and people have biases. Understanding those biases allows me to seek out several points of view to get a better picture of the whole story.*

Body:
While sitting, raise your feet to knee level and rotate your ankles in circles for a count of twenty. This is good for your core and your calves. It also helps build balance and control. Moving your wrists and forearms with the same motion at the same time doubles the calorie burning possibility and tightens up your upper arms.

Mind:
A letter to the advertiser can help change the type of programming you are exposed to. Write letters in a calm, factual manner to increase the likelihood of being read and taken seriously.

Money:
Pay attention to who advertises on television and radio shows that make you angry, or please you. Boycott those that support destructive programming. Visit and buy from those who support good causes. Use your money to change the world.

Joke:
My boss told me, "Don't dress for the job you have, dress for the job you want".
But when I turned up at the office today in Ghostbusters gear, he said I was fired.

Day #40

Never Trust Politicians

Enough said.

Meditation: *Please help me vote for leaders based on what they have done, not what they currently say.*
*I recognize that corporate interests and media outlets define candidates but their **actions** reveal their true character.*
I will learn the history of a candidate before I vote for them because I know their actions affect my life and the lives of my friends, family members and the sustainability of the world.

Body:

Standing facing a wall but try not to use it as you stretch one leg out and up as far behind you as you can stretch comfortably. Relax and repeat on both legs at least twenty times. Balancing as you do this strengthens your core and boosts your muscles tone.

Money:

Donate to politicians who are doing their best for issues that you find important. There is a limit to what you can donate, be aware of it to protect your candidate from bad press.

Mind:

People tend to blink more often when they are lying. Watch a speech by a politician and count the number of times the person blinks on different subjects. You can learn the real truth by watching their eyes.

Joke:
I got a really cute dog and called him Threemiles. It sounds great to say I walk Threemiles twice a day.

Day #41

Vote and Write

You may have seen the bumper sticker that reads, "Don't blame me, I voted for the other guy!"

You *should* blame yourself if you did vote for *THAT* guy. Many voters follow the crowd hoping to choose the candidate that wins so they can say, "My guy won!"

Politics are not horse races. "Winners" often cost us more than we can afford. An elected official decides your future and controls the functions of your government, choose according to your needs.

Many presidential races are won and lost on the issue of abortion but the president is helpless to do anything about that issue. It is handled by the judicial and legislative branches of STATE governments. Voters who don't take time to understand government make foolish choices thinking they are doing something good.

If you vote for a party and find them reneging on promises made, (don't be surprised) do something about it. Visit or call your representative and let them know they are not doing what you elected them to do. Organize petitions, write letters, encourage friends and community groups to write letters or protest.
These are your rights.

Since you are not able to vote in Congress or Parliament you have elected someone who should at least try to represent you. If they don't know what you want, they can't. If they refuse, work to get them out of office.

Meditation: *Please help me to be involved in issues that affect my family, my community and my world. I realize that standing idly by while my government does things I don't agree with is not doing my part as a citizen.*
I will vote for candidates that will help further my goals for the greater good and participate by working for a candidate, writing to my representatives and staying informed on their activities or by protesting injustices.

Body:
Lie on your back and with your arms to your side raise first one leg then the other slowly straight up to the ceiling and back down. Repeat ten to twenty times. Raise both together for a tighter belly!

Money:
It is easier to email or call than to write to Congressman. You can find their email address at whoismyrepresentative.com.

Mind:
Read the voting records to find out where a candidate really stands on issues. If they're never been in office, read about their lives.

Joke:
It's not such a fine restaurant when the waiter says, "Our restaurant's snails are beautiful." and you feel the need to reply, "I know, one of them has just been serving me."

Day #42

Be Aware

Driving down the road one evening in the dead of winter, a motorist noticed that the car in front of him had a finger sticking out of a hole where the tail light should have been.

The motorist's wife used a cell phone to call police who found a nineteen-year-old woman who had been kidnapped by her ex-boyfriend bound and gagged in the trunk of the car wearing only a t-shirt and underwear.

The people driving the car behind the kidnap vehicle were heroes because they were paying attention to their surroundings.

Had they been staring off into space the poor girl probably would have been murdered or may have frozen to death in the cold Tennessee winter.

A young girl whose class had just read a story, in which a tsunami was vividly described, recognized the "fallback phenomenon" that precedes a big wave as it was happening. She alerted her mother who grabbed her siblings and alerted people around her and everyone in the group escaped a killer tidal wave unharmed. Others who weren't near the group weren't so lucky.

What you see could mean the difference between life and death for someone. If faced with a situation in which someone might live or die you don't want to be the one who says, "I wasn't paying attention."

Meditation: *Please help me to be aware of my surroundings. I will make a conscious effort to notice things that may be important.*

Body:

Six Weeks! Weigh yourself. Measure your neck, chest, arms, waist, legs and hips. Take pictures, blog and/or update the chart!

Everyone should be seeing results from your conscious decisions at this point.
You will find it's easier to walk up the stairs, lift things and that you have more energy. This will only improve in the next six weeks.

Money:

On long trips watch for road signs that lead to interesting destinations, Take photos of the hilarious signs instead of visiting tourist traps!

Mind:

Memorize mileage markers on exits you use frequently. When describing directions to someone it is better to say, "Take airport exit 113." than "Take that airport exit." There may be two or three!

Joke:
It remains a puzzle why a bra is singular and panties are plural.

Day #43

Ask Someone to Teach You

There was a group of foreign students in the apartment across the hall of my first apartment. One of the young men sat in the hallway stairs playing his guitar when his full apartment got too noisy. I would open my door to listen to the music that he played. It was different than what I was used to. Lovely. I didn't talk to him, I don't think he spoke English. I didn't speak Spanish.

One day he disappeared. Worried, I knocked on the door across the hallway and young girl answered.

"Hello." she said, "Are you my neighbor?"
"Do you live here?" I asked looking inside for signs of the young man.
"Me and my mom just moved in." she said.

I was sad that I would never hear that music again. If only I had watched to understand that picking style!

Years later I went to a folk festival and toward the end of the event I heard a familiar sound; the hallway music! I followed it to the open door of a workshop and peeked inside. It wasn't my hallway musician but it was definitely the song. I slipped inside and watched his fingers closely. Not quite getting it, I stayed to talk to the instructor.
I asked him where he had heard the song and he told me a Guatemalan college kid in his building played it in the hallway!

Thank goodness *he* thought to ask for instruction. He was happy to show me the tune and now I play it on my own porch stairs when things get too noisy in my house!

There is no harm in taking instruction from a stranger. If you see someone doing something interesting be brave and ask them how to do it. You might be surprised at how willing, even flattered the teacher might be.

Meditation: *Please help me to learn an unusual skill or trick from an unlikely source. I realize that some things that I find interesting will disappear unless I carry the knowledge with me. I will ask for information when I know it can't be found elsewhere.*

Body:

While sitting hold your arms straight out to your sides. Keeping your arms straight bring your hands together in front of you and push them against one another. Open and repeat ten to twenty times.

This is an easy isometric exercise to improve tone in your chest and inner arms. If you make an effort to stretch your arms a little further than straight to your sides, it will also improve flexibility. Again, only stretch as far as is comfortable. Over time you will go further.

Money:

Every summer there are free concerts at many city parks. Look for one near you online. Take along a picnic for a cheap date. It may be the best date you've had!

Mind:

Piano or guitar lessons keep your mind nimble and it's a great hobby you can share with others.

Joke:
An interviewer asked me to characterize myself in 5 words.
I said, "Quite lazy." (I didn't get the job.)

Day #44

Give Anonymously

The headlines read "Mill to Close December 5th" the day Ian saw his father's tears for the first time. He knew the news was bad.

His mother explained that they would have to move from the close-knit mountain town to the city for jobs. Until then, they would give up things like cable television and shopping trips.

Ian didn't mind. He had a drawer full of tractors that were more fun than television but his sister threw a fit! At 16 she expected life to continue as it had without inconvenience.

"No internet will kill my social life!" She screamed.
"No shopping? I'll look like a hobo!"
"You have nice clothes, and everyone is losing their job so you'll all be hobos."
"Are we getting anything for Christmas?
"We can't neglect you but we can't buy expensive things."

Ian listened closely. The young girl stormed up the stairs. Later that evening Ian brought two shoe boxes and handed them to his mother. "Could you help me wrap these?" he asked, as she peeked inside.
"These are your favorite tractors, what are you doing?"
"You said everyone is losing their jobs and Alex and David's dad works at the mills too, right? They don't have tractors. I was thinking I could put these under their Christmas tree and they would think their parents bought them." Mrs. Miller held back tears and hugged her son. Then she got on the phone and called her friends.
Together they organized a "Secret Santa Tree" event. A Christmas tree was put up in a local grocery store. Tags were provided along with pens. Anyone who needed a gift filled out the age and gender of their child and anyone who wanted to help chose a child to buy a gift for. The price limit was $20.

On Christmas Eve, gifts were distributed by Mr. Miller dressed as Santa. Some gifts were new and some were gently used and every house had a fruit and candy basket courtesy of the grocery store. No one knows who gave what, but everyone received something and the town came together in a difficult time to support one another. I've seen similar Secret Santa trees since. It's such a lovely idea, I wish every town had one.

Meditation: *Please help me give without recognition as I am able. I realize the prize is a secret kindness that I can treasure in myself. I will give without waiting for a holiday.*

Body:

While sitting raise your ankles up to the height of your knees. And kick like you are swimming. Repeat at least twenty times. This exercise will tighten saggy knees. By now, some knee fat should be gone and your knees may be looking a little loose. Tightening the muscle under the skin will help keep your legs smooth. Over time your skin will shrink too.

Money:

If you have a limited income look for organizations in your area that take names for Christmas help.
Even if you work, you may qualify. Donate time if you can. Everyone needs help sometimes!

Mind:

Make heirlooms for your family for Christmas! A treasure box or a photo album will be cherished for years and you will enjoy the memories and gain the organizational and/or equipment skills that go with the assembly.

Joke:
An officer stops a car and says: "Congratulations! You are the 1,000,000th car to drive over this bridge – you win $10,000! What will you do with that money?"
The idiot says, "I'll finally get my driver's license!"
The wife cuts in, "Don't listen to him, officer, he's drunk!"
Deaf Granny in the back-seat grumbles, "I knew we shouldn't have taken the stolen car!"

Day #45

Compliment Within Earshot

Adam cringed when he overheard two of his teachers talking during lunch break.

"That Adam Lauder is such a little… (He waited for a word like "stinker".) …gift."

"Adam Lauder?"

"Yes, this morning he came to class on time, sat quietly and turned his test in on time!" The young teacher knew the 7-year-old could hear her. He was listening intently.
"I think I will give him two points this week for cooperation!" She saw the stunned look on her colleague's face. "But he…"

"Shh, you don't have to say it," Positioning herself so he couldn't see that she motioned with her eyes toward the child. "I know. He finally grew into his patience."

That afternoon Adam was especially helpful to his second teacher. He straightened his desk without being told and listened to the lesson intently.

The next day the teacher related to the first that her plan had worked. Adam needed to be noticed when he was good as well as when he was misbehaving.
The boy started to like school quickly and continued his good behavior throughout the year, occasionally slipping but always rewarded for good behavior that earned him compliments and stars on his chart.

The rewards of complimenting someone for a job well done don't just work on children. Everyone appreciates a nod in their direction and, when encouraged, will often go above and beyond what is expected.

Meditation: *Please help me show people that I appreciate them by sharing news of their triumphs with others. I understand that most people work harder when recognized. I will pay someone a public compliment today.*

Body:

Halfway point! You deserve a massage or a manicure. Recruit a friend to trade services or find a spa near you.

Your body is lighter so you may feel like running, but please don't start until you are off of the plan. You're not taking in enough calories to fuel that and risk sickness or injury. When you finish this 90 days there will be plenty of time for running. For now, just walk.

Exercise requires extra protein to limit muscle loss, and complex carbohydrates (an apple or an orange) for energy.

Money:

Take the survey on receipts. Some companies will reward you with free food or discounts!

Mind:

Use words like "industrious" and "meticulous" to describe older kids. If they don't know the meaning they'll look it up and you'll have taught them, as well as complimented them!

Joke:

A guy says urgently to the bartender, "Give me a beer before trouble starts!" He drinks it and orders another, and another. The bartender finally asks, "Hey man, when are you gonna pay for those beers?" The guy answers, "And now the trouble starts!

Day #46

Do Something Nice for a Child

Four-year-old Victoria went to the mailbox with her mom every day. Across the street, Alicia watched how happy she was to help carry it in.
It gave her an idea. She had just found a collection of poems she had written when she was young.
She slipped one into an envelope, addressed it to Victoria, mailed it and waited to watch the following day as the mother and daughter went to the mailbox.

The little girl squealed and bounced up and down as her mother handed her, her OWN mail. She danced around for a while before she opened it in the driveway. Her mother read the poem aloud to her then handed the poem and envelope back. Alicia saw the child hug them close to her as she continued to bounce and dance all the way to the house.

Once a month Alicia anonymously mailed one poem to Victoria. As the years went by, the bouncing evolved to clumsy ballet pirouettes and then to a graceful walk as each poem touched the girl.

On the day she went away to college she knocked on Alicia's door with a full scrapbook of the poems she had saved over the years, a full book that showed Alicia's evolution as a poet and her giving spirit.

"This was your gift to me and I'm keeping it forever. I knew it was you by the lavender smell of your house and I always loved it.... I want you to have this."

She held out a notebook of *new* poems, written first in her childhood scrawl and, as pages progressed, a more refined pen and elegant margin doodles.

Alicia's eyes welled with grateful tears. Now it was she who hugged the poems to her chest.
One minute, once a month made a life changing gift.

Meditation: *Please guide me to the proper way to do something nice for a child. I realize that childhood moments can be remembered for a lifetime. I will do a good deed for a child today.*

Body:

While sitting on the floor with your legs together in front of you, come as close as you can to touching your toes. Raise your arms toward the ceiling and try again. Can you reach farther than last time?

This is great for stretching the muscles around your spine and the backs of your legs. Do not force any stretch but do try to improve your flexibility.

Money:

Little kids don't care about cash.
Letters, specially-packed lunches and yard sale toys are as important to them as expensive gifts. You've seen the many things a child can make from a cardboard box! It's love that matters and money you save!

Mind:

Save fun emails people send to you, and those you write to others! They are a diary of the times and if printed and bound make great gifts!

Joke:
If my spouse laughs at my jokes when I get home, chances are we have guests.

Day #47

Try Harder

Tammy ran around the track with her two best friends. The teacher yelled from across the track, "Pick up the speed girls you have two more laps to go!"

They continued at their pace and the bell rang. "Finish your laps." the teacher snapped. "I'll give you a pass." Tammy was pleased. It meant more time with her friends out of class.

By the time the girls came in four minutes later their teacher had them figured it out.

"Tomorrow we start assigned partners, when your laps are done you can chat." All three girls groaned.

The next day Tammy ran with a guy who sometimes teased her on the bus. She ran until she was winded, walked until she could run, and ran until her laps were done. One of her friends finished soon after. The third friend was paired with a cute boy and wasn't in a hurry.

Each day the teacher paired them with different people. One day Tammy was paired with a girl who didn't like her. "I'm going to whip your ass out there." The girl bragged.

Tammy sprinted to get some distance, but the girl was fast and Tammy had to push herself to stay ahead. She passed her friends twice. Her teacher called to her assistant as Tammy passed them and she ran harder to finish her last lap and finally be done with the grueling exercise.

As she ran past the finish line she heard the assistant, who was also the girls track coach, squeal with joy!

"That's a new gym class record!" she shouted, "Hopefully we have a new track star this year!"

Until the day she found her competitive spirit, Tammy hated running but she had a natural talent for it so she joined the team and helped win a state competition! The lesson Tammy learned was that if you have a reason to try harder you will succeed at whatever you are doing.

Meditation: *Please help me to do my best even at things I find unpleasant. I understand that completing my tasks with quality work will improve my skills. I will give my tasks my best effort today.*

Body:

Sitting on the floor with your legs in front of you and open, get as close as you comfortably can to touching each foot with both hands. This stretches your spine arms and rear thighs for full body flexibility.

Floor work is a good thing for many reasons, there is no danger of falling, getting up and sitting down works muscles you need for almost every activity, and it helps you feel grounded (pardon the pun). Studies have shown that people who connect skin-to-ground regularly feel more at peace.

Money:

Walking is a great way to maintain your cardiovascular system. Maintaining a healthy body saves expensive doctor visits and pharmacy trips.

Mind:

In studies, people who got up and moved between sessions did better on tests than those who stayed in their seats. Get up and move when you feel flustered!

Joke:
I would like to beef up my self-esteem a bit,
but I don't deserve it.

Day #48

Don't Give Up On Your Dreams

Susan started dance class when she was seven. Some of the girls in her class were four years old. She didn't want people to see her in the "baby class", so she asked her mother to put her in tap class where the girls were her age.

She longed for the graceful moves of ballet and asked her mother to reenroll her when she was twelve. At that point, girls in her class were nine years old so Susan quit again fearing she would look like a big oaf.

At seventeen she got a free "older starter" pass so she signed up with another dance school and noticed some of the girls at twelve were naturally gifted so she no matter how she tried, she wouldn't get feature parts.

She quit again, vowing to never take a ballet class again. However, in college she found herself without a class and in need of elective credits so she decided to take one more ballet class.

Her instructor told her she would never be a ballerina although she had great balance and form because at 20 she had started too late. Nonetheless, she finished the class with high marks and didn't dance again until she was 28.

A friend asked her to go along on an audition and she went out of curiosity. For fun she signed up and took a place in line with a lot of younger people in front of the choreographer who watched everyone but her.

She couldn't believe it when she was called back. Tap classes put her over the top. Both friends got a spot in the show and when it closed, Susan decided that her love of dance was stronger than her lack of training or fear of not fitting in. She auditioned until she got another part and learned to dance along the way.

Meditation: *Please help me to give my dreams a chance. I was designed for a purpose, to never try is to question fate. I will put effort into the things that make me happy intentions of making them part of my life.*

Body:

Week seven! Wow, you hung in there!
As every week, weigh yourself and measure your neck, chest, arms, waist, legs and hips. Take pictures, blog and/or update the chart! Deep condition your hair, mask your face and paint your nails. (Men, you should do these things too. A clear polish gives you a sophisticated look.)
Check your supplies and replace those that are too old or spoiled (Moisturizer has a shelf life of 3-6 months.)

Your body is more flexible now. You have been gently elongating and toning your muscles for seven weeks.

Money:

Check online or at your library for videos that teach exercises like dancing and Tai Chi. They're fun!

Mind:

See a dance performance to open your mind to the soothing effect of music and movement.

Joke:
I saw a sign that said: "Caution - Watch for children!"
I thought, how dangerous can these children be?

Day #49

Look for Opportunities

An old man woke one morning to find his town flooded and water lapping at his porch. A fire truck honked outside his door and the firefighters offered to take him to higher ground. "That's okay," the old man responded. "God will take care of me."

The next morning the water had risen above his first floor. The old man looked out a second story window and saw a boat come by. The rescuers offered him a ride. "No thank you," the old man says. "God will take care of me."

Overnight the water continued to rise and morning found the old man sitting on his roof. A helicopter appeared and a rescuer slid down with a basket to help take the old man on board. "I'm okay," the old man reassured him. "God will take care of me."

The old man drowned. When he reached heaven, he saw God and he asked, "Why didn't you save me?"

And God replied, "I sent you a fire truck, a boat and a helicopter. What more do you want?"

Sometimes opportunities are sent to us and we don't recognize them. A lost job might lead you to start a new career, or a broken arm might inspire you to invent a million-dollar gadget for the injured.

Look for the opportunities in things that happen in your life and take advantage of them when you can. You know the old saying. "Opportunity only knocks once."

Meditation: *Please help me to look for signs of unexpected help and use it to my benefit. I understand that they might be disguised as misfortune. I will not turn down any gift from an unusual source.*

Body:

Listen to your body for signs of strain or exhaustion. When you feel exhausted, you burn out.
Exercise is supposed to give you energy not drain you.
It's ok to take a day off, in fact if you don't, you will expose yourself to injury.
Today, just treat your skin to your favorite lotion and allow your body to catch up to you!

Money:

Just because you missed your opportunity to invest in the first shares of Starbucks or Microsoft doesn't mean you can't invest in the next big thing.
Explore your interests. Why not invest in something you use daily and can't live without!

Mind:

Sometimes a chance meeting with someone can be a catalyst for a great new friendship or business opportunity. A real opportunity will feel good, a bad one won't.

Joke:

Web site: "Sorry, your password 25EeffQ@# is not secure."
Cash machine login: "1234": Here's your 1000 dollars.

Day #50

Set a Life Goal

You may have seen a copy of the book *101 Things to Do Before You Die"* by Richard Horne. It's a terrific travel guide of things to do and see around the world.

It's an entertain map of life goals, although many of them are not for me. For instance, I have no desire to attend the Running of the Bulls in Spain but for some, that would be considered a life goal.

A life goal is something that you will recall on your death bed as a shining moment.

Life goals can be as simple as attending a Broadway musical or as complicated as discovering a cure for diabetes. Setting one or a few goals is a big step toward attaining your best life. There is no shame in not completing your life goal but *never trying should be considered a sin*. When you reach one, set another.

Consider your goals to be destinations. When you hear people speak of having no purpose they are describing having no life goals. If you have felt that way yourself, defining a life goal may help set you free of that hopelessness.

There is no shame in setting a goal that seems unattainable as long as it's what you really want to do. There is also no shame in never reaching it. The brush you clear makes the path more accessible to the next explorer.

My life goal is to win The Pulitzer Prize: a lofty goal especially since right now I am only working on *reading* a novel!

Meditation: *Please help me to set goals that are worthy of my time. I understand that I may spend a lifetime working on my goal and that is fine. I know that life is the journey and not the destination. I will set expectations for myself and begin taking steps now to one day reach my goal.*

Body:

While standing, breathe in for ten seconds and out for ten seconds. Raise your hands and tuck in your stomach with each breath and release on exhale. This makes more oxygen available to your cells, relaxes you and help you feel grounded! (Stable, secure.)

Money:

Set a monetary goal for six months from now. Do everything you can to reach that goal short of selling body parts. (Sell plasma if you must!) Goals only work if you work to get to them!

Mind:

Set a goal to learn basic sign language! The alphabet can be learned in a few days, the rest comes with practice. Enlist a partner to study with you and talk to each other silently in public.

Joke:
My boss told me to have a good day.
So I thanked him and went home.

Day #51

Break Goals into Benchmarks

No one can reach their highest goal overnight. (Unless you want to be a millionaire and then win the lottery.) For most of us a goal is something to work toward.

Breaking goals into smaller pieces or levels serves two purposes: it trains you for future success and it gives you the confidence to proceed to the next level.

Samantha could sit on her long hair. Everyone asked her, "How long has it been since you've had a haircut?" She smiled at their curiosity but as the gray began to take over, she knew she'd look better in a shorter style.

She made an appointment but when the day came, she cancelled. She cancelled the second time too and on the third call she explained her fear. The salon owner explained that he had a "four-inch policy". He would never cut more than four inches from any head, ever. Samantha kept the appointment and true to his word the salon manager cut only four inches from her hair.

The difference was remarkable and it took her a few days to get used to her healthier hair.
Three weeks later she requested that he take off four more inches.
Again, he cut only four inches and people began to remark that she looked ten years younger.
Another two cuts and Samantha was finally at the beautiful goal she had set for herself.

She had a cute, easy to manage style. Each cut had given her more confidence until she reached her goal.

Meditation: *Please help me to set small realistic goals on my way to what I want to achieve. I understand that doing a little at a time will give me confidence.*
I will set attainable goals.

Body:

While sitting, stretch your neck to the left and right (not back!) then roll your shoulders in large circles to improve flexibility and relieve stress.
By now you realize that many of these exercises are done sitting so that you can do them at work, on the train or bus or while watching television. They are easy and so beneficial you will do them wherever you are for the rest of your life.

Money:

How much do you spend in a week? Track everything you buy *this* week on a sheet of paper or on your phone. Next week try to spend half that! It's a quick way to save a lot of money!

Mind:

Use your wallet for more than money. Using a tiny font, print the names, addresses and phone numbers of your most important people on a wallet sized card. The next time you're at the post office with a dead phone you will thank yourself!

Joke:
So, I'm already doing 60 in a 30-mph zone
and still this guy is right on my bumper. Then he
blinded me with these fancy blinking blue lights.
The world is full of psychos!

Day #52

Enlist Help

Jennifer had a great idea and she wanted to meet with a manager to discuss it. However, her chain of command was a challenge. Two previous ideas had been stolen by a supervisor who took credit for her work with the explanation that he had developed them with his "crew". (She called him The Pirate.)

She didn't know where to turn. The supervisor monitored her email, the upper manager's secretary wouldn't put her calls or through, and the human resources department was a joke. Sending a letter outside of work would make her look sneaky.

One day a USPS carrier dropped off some packages and Jennifer noticed the manager's name on a registered letter the carrier was on his way to deliver. Realizing that the man would be able to quickly get through his secretary she scribbled out her idea and said, "Would it be possible for you to drop this note off with that envelope?" Her smile convinced him. Ten minutes later she got a call from the man asking her to meet with him to discuss her idea. She convinced him that by using a reliable but relatively unknown internet trick to connect off-site workers he would save the company thousands of dollars a month.

She earned a promotion and was finally able to speak candidly about the supervisor who had kept her from getting the credit she had earned.

The Pirate was keelhauled (reprimanded and transferred).

When a difficult situation arises it's ok to ask outsiders for help. Sometimes it's the only way to get things done. You wouldn't move a piano alone would you? Some things just take two. (or more!)

Meditation: *Please help me the humility to ask for help. I realize that some things can't be done alone. I will ask for help when I need it.*

Body:
Vacuum then spray your mattress once every three months with diluted rubbing alcohol to prevent dust mites and microorganisms from taking over. That mysterious rash may be an allergy to one of them.

Money:
Enlist your friends and family for help getting to your money goal. Contact people who owe you money and call in the loan. Tell them you are trying to raise money and ask for suggestions, they might know something that will get you to your goal overnight!

Mind:
Connect with them through social media. This is your contact list for inside information, fund-raising ideas, and word of mouth advertising!

Joke:
Not every badly unkempt guy is homeless.
It could be that he has a wife and daughter
and only 1 bathroom.

Day #53

Never Break the Chain of Kindness

You've no doubt heard the story of the man whose boss yelled at him so he went home angry and yelled at his wife, who lost her temper and yelled at her son, who felt awful so he yelled at the dog and the poor dog just sat there wondering what the fuss was all about.

What if instead, his boss had said, "We'll have a better day tomorrow."

The man may have brought flowers home for his wife, who gave her son a cookie to share with his dog.

Although there are several lessons to learn from this parable, the most important is that *what you do and say has consequences for others.* With that in mind, the logical thing to do when faced with an unkind person or situation is to disregard the slight and continue to act with kindness toward others.

It's always a good idea to continue a favor chain. A common kindness chain is when people pay for the coffee of the next person in line at a-drive through. Sometimes that chain goes on for hours.
I'm reminded of when my family received a bag of hand-me-down toys and clothes from a cousin. My mother divided them between my siblings and I and then promptly went through our clothes to pass down what we had outgrown to younger cousins.

I felt so good when years later I saw one of my favorite shirts still in circulation on a second generation!

Meditation: *Please help me to remember to pass on the good things that happen to me. I realize that things I say and do can affect more than just the people around me. I will start a chain of kindness by doing a good deed and asking someone to "pass it on."*

Body:

Your clothes are outgrowing you. Take your favorites in for repair, donate, trade or sell your old ones.

As you change, so does your style. Design your fantasy wardrobe online. Once you know what pieces you want, you are more likely to find them when you are casually shopping. Since right now you are trying to save money, look for those pieces at thrift stores first.
The greatest selection is in the smaller sizes. Soon you will be able to choose from what you really want.

Money:

Pay your debts, especially to friends. Some may need the money but may be embarrassed to ask. Clear your debts and you will feel better and be free to receive new favors and a lot of good will!

Mind:

If you owe someone a letter, write it by hand today. Writing by pen stimulates areas of your brain that typing or talking on the phone don't. Also, it's classy.

Joke:
A Priest, a Rabbi and an Imam walk into a bar.
The bartender looks at them suspiciously and says,
"Is this some kind of a joke?"

Day #54

Try Something Again

Sherry got a beat-up guitar when she was ten. It was cracked and missing strings but she took it outside where she wouldn't disturb anyone and discovered all the different sounds she could make with it.
She wanted to learn to play, but without strings, a teacher or instruction books, (The internet had not been introduced.) it collected dust until her parents donated it to charity.

As a young adult, she met a man who played guitar and he showed her a few chords, but he was an impatient teacher and she gave up in frustration.

One day she heard an interview with George Thorogood saying he couldn't believe how lucky he was that his music was being accepted by audiences. "I only knew three chords and I was playing clubs!" Something in Sherry awakened. Three chords?

She borrowed a guitar from a friend and went to the library for an instruction book. She sat with that book and played three chords; D, G, and C until she could switch with ease. Then she tried those chords on different frets up and down the neck of the guitar. All at once she realized she was making music! Her success led to her desire to learn more chords and later, to write her own music. She recently recorded a CD of her music.

It's never too late to do something you want to do. If you have given up on something, I encourage you to try it again. You may be a different person than you were when you first attempted. You've heard the old adage, "If at first you don't succeed try, try again."

Meditation: *Please help me to keep an open mind about things at which I may have failed in the past. I realize that changes in my character or technology might make it possible to succeed where I failed before. I will answer that nagging call and try again.*

Body:
Stretch before bed each night to relax your body and get nourishing blood flowing to repair damage.
Stretch when you wake up to restore energy and prepare your muscles for the work ahead.

Money:
You might be surprised at how easy it is to make your own music. If you own no musical instruments try music making software or websites. With some, all you have to do is assemble pre-recorded clips and add your voice!

Mind:
Reading music exercises our minds and helps us understand and follow multistep processes. There are free instructional videos online to teach you are your own pace.

Joke:
If you start to think I talk too much, just tell me. We'll talk about it.

Day #55

Experiment with Food

I had never tried Indian food. (The most exotic food I knew about was lasagna!) The man with the interesting accent and sharp black tunic was patient with me when he asked, "Do you want your food a one, a five or in between?"

"I only want one," I said. "I'm not that hungry."

"No, I'm asking do you want your Vindaloo mild (one) or do you want it very spicy (five) or somewhere in between?"

"Oh! I think I had better try a one, please." I blushed at my ignorance. The smell of the restaurant was incredible. I didn't recognize any of the fragrances except the cinnamon in my tea. It smelled of spices that made the cinnamon seem as exciting as oatmeal by comparison.

When the food came I was very pleased that I had chosen a "one". The new spices were breathtaking. Literally. I breathed them in. My dinner companion had chosen a three and he was suffering.

The next time I went, I tried a green curry, at two, it was even better! The third time I tried Biryani (three) and loved it too!

Since then I have gone out of my way to try food at Thai, Mexican, German, Chinese, and Irish restaurants.

I have my favorites at each but I'll never forget the first time I had to decide between a one and a five.

Meditation: *Please help me to be brave enough to experience something outside of my normal. I understand that I have seen very little of the vast experiences that are available. I will seek out new food, new recipes, new restaurants, and new groceries.*

Body:

Week eight! Weigh yourself. Measure your neck, chest, arms, waist, legs and hips. Take pictures, blog and/or update the chart!
Keeping track of progress gives you solid proof that you can do it.
You've come this far and that is amazing.
If you've reached your goal, congratulations!
If you're still moving toward it, look how far you've come! Only four weeks to go!

Money:

Reinvent a recipe you love with new spices or sauces or invent your own recipes!
Learning to cook can save you a lot of money and impress your friends.

Mind:

Ask your family for old recipes and make them. The smells will take you back to your childhood and the experience is something you can share with your own children or friends.

Joke:
I wish I could go to Mykonos again."
"Wow, you've been to Mykonos?"
"No, but I've wished it before."

Day #56

Exercise Reason

I was visiting a friend with two little girls when her husband came home late drunk and tripped over the older daughter's coat on the floor.

"Heather!" he bellowed from his hands and knees, "You get this coat off the floor right now or I swear I will beat you until your sister hurts!"

Heather hung the coat on the hook from which it had fallen then ran to her room and slammed her door. The coat fell back to the floor.

I was afraid for the little girls. Their mother assured me that his bark was worse than his bite and they would be fine but I stuck around longer than I had intended to be sure. (I twisted her hook back to shape on my way out.)

I was appalled that a man would speak to anyone with such spite for such a small problem and I was relieved that it was only talk. I know so many stories of child abuse and neglect that my "shackles were up" at the thought of it.

He would have gotten a better result from his daughter if he had asked her to pick it up nicely or even better, picked it himself. (*He* had knocked it down!)

The next time I was over, the girls' now three months sober father came home from work. "Whose books are these? Please move them." he called. This time it was the younger daughter's and she shuffled over to hug him and scoop up the books. Heather followed her sister and hugged her father too. No problems here.

Although both girls were safe, in many cases women, elderly people, and children are not safe from sudden rage, especially when there is alcohol involved.

I urge anyone who knows they have a temper to think when they feel their blood boil. "Do I have a reason, to be unreasonable?" The answer is always no.
Think before yelling at someone. Never be violent.

Meditation: *Please help me to control my temper and exercise reason when I am upset. I realize that I will get a better result if I keep my cool. I will breathe quietly and calm down before blowing my top.*

Body:

Planking requires no equipment and no extra space. Lie face down on a yoga mat or comfortable surface. Pretend you are a solid wood plank and go fully rigid while resting your upper body on your elbows and your lower body on your toes.

This exercise involves core muscles. It improves strength, balance and endurance. Hold for a count of five, then increase in increments of five until you can hold a plank for a minute. It's harder than you think!

Money:

Threatening letters seldom work when asking for a refund or price reduction. Be clear about the problem ask for what you want and show patience for best results.

Mind:

Children who have been verbally abused by their parents pass it on to their children. Be aware of your own unfriendly language to help kids feel safe.

Joke:
I saw a poster today, somebody was asking "Have you seen my cat?" So, I called the number and said that I didn't. - I like to help where I can.

Day #57

Be Patient

In Tibet there is rumored to be a temple near the top of a mountain that can only be accessed by walking up a thousand stone steps. Only those who have the patience to climb those stairs can enter the temple.

There is a discipline to patience that serves us in everyday life. Every masterpiece you see is a testament to the artist's patience. This is why when we look at a piece by Michelangelo we stand in awe. Who do *you* know that would be patient enough to lie in a hot building on their back for years painting on a ceiling?

Patience is seen by some religions as mastery of self. In Western culture, there is a declining respect for patience. When a leader can't get what he wants by asking, he takes it anyway, beginning a chain reaction that angers and alienates the world.

A tiny Macedonian nun named Agnes watched a group of children pick through trash for food. She wanted to change their standard of living so she wrote letters and attended many tedious meetings, plodding away at her goal until years after she began her journey, thousands of children had been fed, clothed, and educated. For eternity she will be known as "Mother Teresa"

From the very top of our government to the meekest among us, patience is the key to shaping the world.

Meditation: *Please help me exercise patience in my everyday life. I realize that some things take more time than I would expect. I will use the time I spend waiting to think of things ways to change things for the better.*

Body:

While sitting in a swivel chair, keep your upper body in position by holding onto your desk or a table and swivel your lower body to the right and to the left only as far as is comfortable. This is a waist whittling exercise that can be done at your desk any time. You can isometrically work your arms too if you hold tightly to your desk as you twist.

Money:

Don't panic if your investments seem to tank when the market goes low. Unless you need the money to live, don't panic sell. Give investments a reasonable time to recover.

Mind:

When patience is threatening to escape take a deep breath and count backward from nineteen. Often by the time you get to ten you will be able to speak in a calm and reasonable manner.

Joke:
Why did the CEOs building burn to the ground?
His secretary was out. There was no one to call 911!

Day #58

Learn About Other Cultures

Jonathan was sent to the Middle East to interview administrators of a school for children orphaned by war.

He was shown to a room where the kids would soon be sitting for a photo session. The principal entered the room just as Jonathan clumsily pulled out his expensive camera. He held out his available left hand to shake the man's hand. The principal snorted and pointed to a chair.

Jonathan sat and got comfortable, putting one foot comfortably on his other knee. The principal and the interpreter both gasped at once and the principal hurried out of the room. A teacher was sent in to tell him that the session was cancelled, he would have to conduct the interview by phone.

Jonathan was stunned. He had travelled thousands of miles to speak to the children. What had happened? The interpreter hurried Jonathan out of the building and explained that by shaking with his left hand and by showing the principal the bottoms of his shoes he had deeply insulted the man.

Repairs had to be made. It took days of volunteer work and apologies to get Jonathan back in the room to a still-chilly reception.

We should be aware of the customs and traditions of other cultures. It pays to know for instance that Yom Kippur, not Hanukah, is the most important Jewish holiday. It is a day of fasting and prayer.
Devout Muslims pray a short prayer five times a day, and Indian people of many faiths do not eat beef. A guest or host of a different culture will appreciate your knowledge and acceptance of their way of life even if you don't subscribe to it yourself.

When you know that you will be in the company of someone with a different culture it is best to read about that culture beforehand to avoid unnecessary conflicts.

Meditation: *Please help me to have respect for people who were raised with customs different than my own. My habits may seem strange to them too. I will learn about someone else's life and use the lesson to better understand the world and my place in it.*

Body:

While sitting, rotate your shoulders in wide then small circles then wide again at least twenty times.
This great stress buster can be done daily but should be done at least once a week to help you avoid future shoulder injuries.

Money:

Study before investing in foreign funds or markets.
There are a million scammers trying to convince you that you are missing the greatest opportunity ever.
You may have no recourse if they take your money.

Mind:

Practice your foreign language skills whenever you can.
Visit a restaurant owned by someone of the language's ethnicity.
Sit near the kitchen and immerse yourself in the kitchen chatter. Use the language if you can.

Joke:
Why couldn't the contractor's nephew change a light bulb?
He kept breaking them with the hammer.

Day #59

Think It Through

"I want that last piece of chocolate cream pie but there is that guy looking at it. I should scoop it up before he does. He's a pretty tough-looking guy. What if he gets upset and holds a grudge? What if he starts looking for reasons to fight and we have to go outside and settle it. He'll kill me!

I really want that pie. What if he gets it? Then I'll be in a bad mood. I'll hold a grudge and no matter what he does, I won't like him. I might end up saying or doing something to upset him and he is a really big guy.

Hey, there's a knife. That's a big piece of pie. What if I cut it in half and take only one half? Then he gets pie, I get pie and everyone is happy!"

Sometimes thinking through to a possible conclusion can lead to a positive result for everyone. In this case two people got something that both wanted and no one got killed.

It takes longer to read something than it does to think it. The above "thought process" takes 30 seconds to read but five seconds to think. Five seconds in this case may have saved hours of anguish.

It's better to take a few seconds to contemplate a decision than a day or even a lifetime to regret it.

Meditation: *Please help me to think things through before making decisions that could end badly. I realize that there may not be time to consider all conclusions but at least two alternatives will help me make a better decision. I will contemplate important decisions from different perspectives before committing to them.*

Body:

While sitting, raise your feet to knee level and rotate your ankles in circles for a count of forty; twenty in one direction and twenty in the other to tightens your thighs, strengthen your ankles and get blood flowing in your legs.

Money:

Before you give someone your money, ask yourself where it will end up? Is it to enrich the world or the CEO? Use your money where you know it will help and you won't miss it as much.

Mind:

Try not to watch a trailer before seeing a movie. Sometimes trailers give most of the best parts away. Movies were meant to be experienced without expectation or anticipation!

Joke:
I like to sleep naked, which is why the flight attendant didn't ask for the blanket back.

Day #60

Put Yourself in Their Shoes

Joe Walsh, the famous guitarist from *The Eagles,* took his daughter to a park and she was thirsty. They looked for a water fountain and when they got to it the little one wanted to "do it herself!" but the fountain was too high. Joe picked up his daughter and helped her get a drink while allowing her to do as much as she could herself. That sweet moment stayed with him.

His daughter was tragically killed in an accident and Joe was beyond devastated. As a memorial to her he built a tiny water fountain in that park that little kids can use with no help.

Joe has the increasingly rare ability to see things from another person's perspective. He has so much faith in his audience that he named one of his albums, *"You Bought It, You Name It."*

Perspective is useful when you see a car pull into a handicapped space and watch the driver get out and run into the store. Instead of thinking, "Hey, he's not handicapped!" realize it might be a good day for a man who, when his multiple sclerosis is active, may not be able to walk at all. He may also be going inside to pick up his mother who uses a walker or driving for someone who is sitting in the back seat waiting for him to go in and get a wheelchair.

Seeing things from someone else's perspective serves you by helping you deal with irrational anger.

Drinking from the little water fountain will help you to realize that not everyone is as lucky as you are!

Meditation: *Please help me to try to see from someone else's perspective in order to understand why certain things are necessary. I know that different people have different needs. I will imagine myself as the person I might unfairly judge and try to help them instead.*

Body:

Place your hands against the wall and move your body away from it to arm's length. Lean and touch your head to the wall without moving your feet. Only stretch as far as is comfortable. This exercise lengthens your Achilles tendon and prevents plantar fasciitis, a painful heel condition that is a result of injury or activity. Try it the next time your heels hurt or any time you need to stretch the muscles in your calves.

Money:

In lieu of funeral flowers, plant a tree in someone's name. A living tree is a fitting tribute to a life, that won't end up in a trash bin. Often a park will allow you to place small plaque or even a bench in their honor.

Mind:

Write your own eulogy. Include things you plan to do in the future that you would like to be known for. Thinking of how you want people to remember you is a good way to set future goals and evaluate your progress as a good person.

Joke:
I broke my personal record for a 100-yard dash: I'm nearly on 55 yards.

Day #61

Advise Your Best Friend

Melissa told me she was thinking of leaving her husband. They argued all the time. She stood between him and the television, handed him an empty plate he had just finished and told him to take it to the kitchen. She reminded him to walk the dog, mow the lawn and take some things to the garage while she was gone. He was engrossed in a basketball game and he just nodded. She frowned and said loudly, "Why do they never pay attention to us?" I told her we were late and we should hurry to meet our friends for lunch.

When we reached the restaurant, the friends were waiting, one was switching her chair for a "steadier" one. We had a long lunch during which we discussed our relationships. The steady-chair friend repositioned her place setting and rearranged the flowers. She sent her salad back because the tomatoes were not ripe enough and called the waitress an idiot under her breath. She was upset because her husband played golf with friends all weekend, the only time they both had to spend together.

Melissa who had watched our friend fuss over everything, chimed in. "If you weren't so bitchy he might be nicer to you!" I looked her in the eye and said, "He might just want to enjoy his favorite sport during the peak of the season." She blushed.

She had just given our friend the answer to her earlier question.

Often when something is bothering you, think about what you would say to a friend if they asked you the same question. You are your friend, right?

You probably know your best friend better than anyone else but who knows YOU better than anyone else? You!

Meditation: *Please help me to remember that I already know the answer to my questions. I will approach my problems as if they are someone else's and look at them with a fresh eye toward improving myself.*

Body:

To relax in tense situations or when you feel overwhelmed, tighten first your face then release it, then your neck, release. Tighten your hands, release. Your arms, release. Chest, release. Stomach, back, bottom, legs then feet. Release.
This helps soothe tension you didn't know you had. Most people find that by releasing tension in their muscles, they also release it from their mind.
This exercise is great for helping you to get to sleep as well!

Money:

Ask your friends where they invest. Some may have horror stories that will keep you from making the same mistakes. Some will have great tips.

Mind:

Write out your problems. Now look them over as if they belonged to your best friend. What would you advise a friend do about them?

Joke:
My dog used to chase people on a bike a lot.
It got so bad, I had to take his bike away.

Day #62

Move Past Your Childhood

Although psychiatrists worldwide agree that many mental problems develop in childhood, they also agree that most common problems that we face can be solved by exploring the past and moving on.

Angela was forty-seven and her house looked like a museum warehouse. In every nook, she had boxes of knick-knacks and chachkas. It was interesting but there was so much of it!
Her friends talked her into having a sale and agreed help.

When the time came to organize for the sale four people showed up with price stickers, bags, boxes and the energy to sort it out. Angela panicked and backed out.

"I know these things aren't necessary, but I love them!"
"My mother never bought me anything that wasn't necessary." She declared. "So, I bought it for myself."

I picked up a picture of Angela as a teenager. She was wearing a pair of stilts. "Who bought those stilts?" I asked.
"My father," She replied with her head down. "He always made sure I had what I wanted."
"So, even though your mother didn't buy unnecessary things, your father did."
"Yes but...'
"So, you always got what you wanted but not from your mother. Were your parents divorced when you were little?
"Yes, seven so?"
"So she knew you would get those things from him and didn't waste her very limited money on them."
"OH!"

As we packed boxes, she talked about how her mother alway listened when she needed her and took her places while her father bought her things to keep her occupied. The things she kept were really about her father, not her mother. Having things meant love to her. Forty years of collecting had buried her in a substitute for affection.

By the end of the day we had taken out five boxes. Many more ahead. These things take time.

Meditation: *Please help me understand the motivation of my parents when I'm tempted to blame them for my problems. I realize that no one is perfect and that most parents don't realize they are making mistakes. I will forgive my parents and live as an independent adult.*

Body:

Lie on your back and with your arms to your sides, raise first one leg then the other slowly straight up toward the ceiling and back down. Repeat ten to twenty times. Raise both together for a tighter belly! Floor exercises can't be done at the office (unless you have a private office, in which case you have no excuse) but they can be done on your living room, bedroom or even your kitchen floor.

Money:

Everything has changed since your parents taught you about money but some of their advice still holds true. Get an education, work hard, pay your bills, save a 10% of every paycheck, and give to charity if you can.

Mind:

Think about the circumstances of your birth. How old were your parents, what sort of education did they have? What were their difficulties? How did their parents treat them? Understanding can lead to forgiveness and even gratitude.

Joke:
"You know how it is in life. One door closes
– that means another door opens."
"Great, but you either fix it or
I'm expecting a deep discount on this car!"

Day #63

Take Responsibility for Failures

The mess on the hallway wall spanned six feet from the bathroom to the kitchen. Ellen stifled a scream when she saw it and tried to control her voice when she yelled, "Who did this in the hallway?!"

Silence. It had been a bad day and tears of frustration welled up in her eyes as she viewed the mess through them.
"Hey! I want to know who did this to the hallway, right this minute!" She yelled again. Almost getting control of her eyes and voice she added. "Now."

Her tiny four-year-old opened her bedroom door and peeked around it. Her little sister peeked out from behind her. Both of their hands were smeared with lotion, powder and several colors of eye shadow.

"I did that mama. The preschooler whispered guiltily.
"And MEE!" squealed the younger child with pride.

The heavy tears ran down Ellen's face to a smile of pride for her older child. She had admitted her guilt with no regard for consequence. She was also proud of her younger daughter's satisfaction in her work.

She realized neither child had known it was wrong but both were willing to cop to the action even when they found out. They cleaned the wall together and Ellen made them promise never to do it again. Then they went to the kitchen to make a new mess. A cake!

We all make mistakes. We fail at things, we make messes and sometimes we upset others. Only when we admit our mistakes, learn from them and decide not to make them again can we "clean the wall" and start something new.

Meditation: *Please help me to take responsibility for my actions and learn from them. I realize mistakes are lessons. I will clean up things I've messed up and begin anew.*

Body:

While sitting, hold your arms straight out to your sides, then bring your hands together and push them against one another. Open and repeat ten to twenty times. To do the other side of your arms, stand with your back against a wall. Raise your arms to your sides then push yourself away from the wall using the backs of your hands. Or press the backs of your hands against a door frame. Repeat ten to twenty times.

Money:

Paint your walls in scrubable latex and messes like the one described above won't require an expensive paint job. When remodeling, go for things that will save money long term.

Mind:

What are some things you would do differently if you could? Would you be the same person now if you undid them? What would you have missed? What other consequences would have occurred?

Joke:
In a boomerang shop: "I'd like to buy a new boomerang please. Also, can you tell me how to throw the old one away?"

Day #64

Take Credit for Success

A group of students made posters for an International Fair. Four students worked on the welcome sign that featured Spanish dancers, German horn players, and French chefs. The poster was nice and a local car dealer who was a sponsor noticed it got a good idea. He called the art teacher and asked him if he could arrange to hire the student who had painted the dancers. He was looking for someone to paint his window for a Cinco de Mayo sale. He was willing to pay $200 because he liked the style.

The teacher told the class about the call and asked who had painted the dancer. The shy girl who painted it didn't speak up in class but she had intended to tell the teacher after class. Before she could do that another girl spoke up and took credit for it.

She took the job and painted a disappointing dancer on the dealer's window. True to his word the dealer gave her $200 then hired a professional to scrape it off and no one saw it or ever knew that the real artist, who had been bullied relentlessly for her hand-me-down clothes, could have used that money more than anyone.

Some very good ideas are lost due to someone's unwillingness or inability to promote their own work. Taking credit for your successes can lead to better ones in the future!

Meditation: *Please help me to accept praise and recognition when it given. I realize that I have something to contribute to the world. I will make my work available and proudly tell people about it.*

Body:

While sitting raise your ankles up to the height of your knees. Repeat at least twenty times. You've probably noticed by now that these exercises are repeating.

Quick Weight loss causes sags and we want to keep our knees and upper arms from becoming floppy. If your skin isn't keeping up with you, try massaging nightly with body lotion! Remember, just like a deflated balloon your skin will continue shrinking with time, meanwhile a little loose skin can be easily covered with clothes. Fat really can't!

Money:

When you find something that works, duplicate it! Found a pair of timeless shoes that fit perfectly? Buy two pairs and when one wears out you will not have to search endlessly for another pair.

Mind:

Give yourself credit. When you do something noteworthy, write a press release and send it to your local paper. They often look for local "fillers". The recognition you get will spur more successes!

Joke:
"Doctor, you remember this strengthening solution you prescribed me yesterday?"
"Yes, what's the matter?"
"I'd like to use it but I can't open the bottle!"

Day #65

Control Your Feelings

My father's face was red and the veins in his forehead were purple! His hands and head were shaking, he was yelling at me so loudly I couldn't understand what he was saying. I could smell his breath he was so close and when he raised his hands toward my neck, I was certain he meant to kill me. I didn't breathe. I couldn't think. All I could do was stand in front of him. The rest of my family stood outside my open door and watched with varying degrees of terror and fascination. I was grateful that they were there as witnesses, just in case.

Seconds passed but it felt like hours. My father screamed until his voice cracked and snapped him back to his senses. He pushed me and I fell back against a wall, then he turned and walked away.
It was my first encounter with rage. I was 13. It left quite an impression. I avoided him whenever I could.

My own children make me angry sometimes. However, the lesson I learned that day was that no amount of anger is worth a lifetime of distance.

Loss of control can lead to bad feelings, physical violence, and even accidental death.

Being in control of your feelings allows you to get your point across in a manner that encourages feedback and change. It allows both parties to continue to communicate and solve problems with love.

Meditation: *Please help me to control my feelings of rage and anger even though I recognize that I have a right to feel them. I realize that things I do in a state of rage can have consequences that last long after the anger. I will remove myself from a situation before I let rage or disappointment control me.*

Body:

On your hands and knees lift one leg, toe pointed, up to the height of your bottom (no further) slowly lower your knee to the ground or if you can up to your chest! Repeat ten times per leg. Bust that butt!

Money:

When you buy something for which maintenance is becoming expensive, don't sink more money into it. Sell it, (even if it's at a loss) and move on!

Mind:

Keep a positive attitude.
Instead of thinking "That guy is a jerk and I'd like to punch him in his face." think, "What views do we share?" Then work on getting him to that common ground or walk away. No punching.

Joke:
I thought I'd tell you a good time-travel joke,
but you didn't like it.

Day #66

Be Aware of Hatred

We don't often recognize dangerous sociopaths but they exist all around us.

A case in point is Westboro Baptist church. Members of WBC are encouraged to picket the funerals of those who have died in battle or of deadly diseases.

Their leader has died but the church has made no apologies for his hatred and they still picket events to get publicity and donations for their church. Members involve their children in their protests, encouraging a new generation of small-minded citizens.
Most legitimate churches have stood against them.

There are other US groups that are formed on hatred such as the Ku Klux Klan and the Arian Nation. Most of their members were also indoctrinated at a young age.

You may never have to deal with these organizations but you will no doubt be among people who think as they do. In many cases they are poor, unemployed and desperate for a reason to feel like they are better than someone else.

They are dangerous. To ignore them is to encourage them, to accept their thoughts is to become them. It's best not to keep their company.

If Fred Phelps had marched alone, he would have been fined or jailed for hate speech, but his group continues profit from it.

Surround yourself with loving intelligent people, be loving and intelligent yourself. Change begins within.

Meditation: *Please help me to recognize hatred and work against it. I realize bigotry is often perpetuated by people who blame others for their lack of success. I will not support people who use hatred to motivate others, instead show people how to rise above it.*

Body:

While sitting on the floor with your legs together, come as close as you can to touching your toes. You will find you can reach even further. If you can now touch your toes, raise your arms toward the ceiling as high as you can and repeat ten to twenty times.

Money:

DON'T give money to organizations that promote hate. If your church preaches hate, leave it, if your company discriminates, get a new job. Investigate companies before investing your clean money. When we all help each other, everyone succeeds.

Mind:

Can you recite the preamble to the constitution? How many items on the Bill of Rights can you remember? Try to memorize them, they may be useful even if you don't like to talk politics. They are YOUR rights, you should know them.

Joke:
I read of an outbreak of an intestinal virus, in which 9 out of 10 infected suffered from diarrhea. I can't stop thinking about that tenth person who enjoyed it.

Day #67

Explore Your Biases

We are all biased. Biases are based on preference and perspective. (Especially when it comes to dating.)

However, there is another reason for biases that goes beyond preference. It's called *implicit* bias: the unconscious attribution of particular qualities to a member of a certain social group

Englishmen can't show emotion. (Ever watched an English football match?) Black men are fast. (I'd bet on Weird Al in a race against Cedric the Entertainer.) Irish people are drunks. (Someone, tell Bono he's doing it wrong.)
None of those statements are true, but they are so widely disseminated that you recognize them. Since we know they're not true, *why would you believe any of the other prejudice stereotypes*?

Implicit bias leads to prejudice and prejudice makes life harder for people who were born female, Mexican, Irish, Jewish, black, brown, handicapped etc. ... really anything but a middle aged white European, Canadian, Australian or American male.

Nonetheless, Nelson Mandela (African), Bono (Irish), George Burns (Jewish), Mother Theresa (Female) and Sammy Davis Jr. (Black, Jewish, and legally blind!) all overcame prejudice to make the world a better place!

Good people do well regardless of what bad people think of them. Be a good person.

Go places where people of all cultures mingle and try to see the world through different eyes.

Meditation: *Please help me to recognize the reasons I have believed fallacies and release those biases. I may have been wrong about a group of people based on what I have been exposed to. I will investigate the positive side of all people.*

Body:

Sitting on the floor with your legs open as far as is comfortable, try to touch one toe and then the other with the opposite hand. (Your left foot with your right hand and your right foot with your left hand.) This is to keep you limber and less prone to injury!

Money:

Look into investing in microloan funds. They loan to people in Third World countries where traditional loans are not available to help start small businesses. Returns are often higher than interest rates and you're doing good in the world!

Mind:

Laughter is a means of communicating to strangers that we are harmless. What does your laugh convey about you? Do you stifle it? Do you belly laugh? Allow yourself to laugh to relieve stress and heal your body!

Joke:
Why do you never see elephants hiding in trees? Because they're really, really good at it.

Day #68

Be Merciful

It's tempting to call the manager on the guy who gave you fish instead of the cheeseburger you ordered.

You would like to lay on your horn when someone cuts you off in traffic.

You want to yell at the woman who pays for twenty-five dollars' worth of groceries with change, but in all cases, it is the wrong thing to do.

Calling the manager may get the kid fired, but won't teach him about quality service, and it may cause his friends to spit on your next burger.
Ask nicely for a replacement.

Honking at a bad driver could cause an accident or give him a reason to hurt you.
Stay calm, this moment will mean nothing very soon.

The woman in line may be spending the last money she has to feed her kids. Why add to her enormous stress?

Mercy is a marvelous thing to carry. Saying to the kid in the fast food place, "I was new once too." might help him want to do a better job.

Giving the bad driver a little more space might save a life, make traffic move along more quickly and lower both of your insurance rates.

Talking to the people around you in line will make time go faster, help the cashier with the stress of the job and might turn a stranger into a friend!

When you are tempted to "shoot the idiot" think about how you would feel if you were that person.

A smart person errs on the side of mercy in all things.

Meditation: *Please help me to show mercy in situations where I want to act brashly. I realize there are unusual circumstances in some cases. I will act the way I would want to be treated in the same situation.*

Body:

Today's exercise is for your mind as well.
Remember calisthenics? We all remember jumping jacks, sit-ups and push-ups, but there are more.
Do one or two of as many as you remember to get your blood pumping. How silly were they as compared to today's exercises! They are still a great way to stay in shape and to help you remember elementary school!

Money:

Being a merciful driver will save you money on insurance and speeding tickets. See if your insurance company has a good driver discount, some offer a "safe driver course" that could save you hundreds of dollars a year.

Mind:

Read a word backwards. Try a sentence, a paragraph. The act of mentally flipping words and sounding out the result helps us to think quickly and read faster. Also it sounds funny when you do it outloud.

Joke:

Secretary: "Doctor the invisible man is here, should I send him in? He doesn't have an appointment."

Doctor: "Tell him I can't see him."

Day #69

Be Honest but Kind

If the jeans look horrible, there is no good answer to, "How do I look in these jeans?"
There is only honesty and a lie.

There are many ways to be honest. A tactful person can talk someone into changing clothes and make it seem as if it was their idea!

"How do I look in these jeans?"
"Jeans? I thought you wanted to look sexy!" (professional, serious, hot, sporty) I loved those black pants. Remember when you wore those? What else do you have?"
"You don't like these on me?"
"I love the black pants."

It's a cop out to say, "You look fine."
If someone feels self-conscious, they won't enjoy themselves which could ruin your good time too. (Also, then you have to look at those awful jeans all night!)

If someone else is brave and honest enough to tell the person about the problem later, they will never trust *your* word again.

Honesty is important and tact is a way to be honest without offending.

Meditation: *Please help me to find a way to tell someone bad news without being rude or offensive by offering an alternative. I understand that bad news is made worse by a lie. I will try to be honest but kind.*

Body:

Listen to your body for signs of strain or exhaustion. If you did all the calisthenics yesterday, you may be sore in places no one has seen. Take a day off, drink hot tea and relax. Today might be a good day to read, listen to music, or do anything that soothes your mind and allow you to heal. You can exercise when you're finished with this program. In fact, you will want to!

Money:

Don't lie to your spouse about bills. If they don't know where the money goes, they can't help fix problems. Eventually the truth will come out anyway.
Be honest and work together.

Mind:

Try to read a book a week, not just during this program, but for the rest of your life. The books don't have to be long, or informative. You can read romance novels if you like. Reading does great things for your brain. (I suggest The Mend by T. Linsay Cole for adventurous readers.)

Joke:

Why did the physics teacher break up with the biology teacher? There was no chemistry.

Day #70

Be Satisfied with Less

Mike told me about two homeless men he encountered on the Seattle waterfront:

One was a pretty nasty guy. He pushed a little cart stacked high with clothes, a radio, a sleeping bag, groceries and magazines he collected from the terminal's benches. He cursed at people who got too close, especially in the evening.

The second man always said, "Hello." and he always smiled although he only had a few teeth to flash. He never carried anything but food and water and sometimes a hip bag full of magazines he sold for money. One day I saw him sleeping at a table so I put a sandwich in front of him and hurried away.

Weeks later I saw him at the landing. He was on the top deck feeding seagulls. He smiled when he saw me. I said hello and asked him why he was always in such a good mood and he said. "I don't have any reason not be!"

Mike liked that answer and thought about it as he walked away. As he was leaving the man called out "Thanks for the sandwich!" (He didn't know he had been seen.)

The next time I passed the grumpy man I asked him why he was so mean to everyone. "People are always trying to steal my stuff!" He yelled. "I can't even sleep because damn thieves will steal everything!

"Why do you need all that stuff?" I asked.

"This is all I have in the whole world!" he yelled back. I wanted to ask him more questions but was afraid to make him mad, so I walked away. As I left he called out, "Hey! Do you have any spare change?!

Things didn't mean anything to the first man; he found ways to fulfill his needs, he didn't need to own anything to be happy, he even shared his spare food with animals.

The second man held so tightly to his belongings that he missed out on treasures that might have come his way: sandwiches from strangers, the gratitude of animals and the comfort of a good night's sleep.

Meditation: *Please help me to try to realize that too many possessions are a burden. I realize that if my things cause me stress I don't need them. I will value my possessions less and people more.*

Body:

Ten weeks, can you believe it?
Weigh yourself. Measure your neck, chest, arms, waist, legs and hips. Look in the mirror. You should see big changes. Take pictures, blog and/or update the chart! Admire yourself. You've done a great thing.
Try to find at least three things you love about your body. You can work on the things you want to change later, but for now, look at your incredible progress.

Money:

Reducing your dependence on possessions frees you to enjoy your life. Sell or give away what you don't use. Refuse to buy what you don't need.

Mind:

What would you save if you your house was on fire? Those are the things that matter. Explore your fire choices to see what's most important in your life.

Joke:
Don't be upset when a bird poops on your head.
Be happy that horses can't fly.

Day #71

Don't Always Strive to be the Alpha

You've probably seen the bumper sticker that reads, "If you're not the lead dog, the view never changes."

It's true but that lead dog has to be the eyes for the entire team and he can't enjoy the view.

Each dog behind him pulls as they can, and they have the freedom to look around at the view from the side. They feel the occasional relaxing of the harness as others dogs pick up the slack the lead dog pulls and pulls, constantly looking for the best footholds and ways to avoid obstacles and hazards in his path. Poor fellow, even when he is resting he must be on his guard, for the other dogs understand that he is the favorite and they will jump on any opportunity to take his place.

CEOs are afforded many perks and they live like kings. But the majority of those who spent a lifetime avoiding the pitfalls of being a leader and constantly climbing the company ladder deal with too much stress and only get to enjoy it for a short time before succumbing to disease, corruption or misfortune.

Instead of striving to be lead dog it is better to pull along with those beside you, making progress and friends. If your networking skills and the friends you make along the way propel you upward it was meant to be, take advantage of your well-deserved momentum. You may get your turn in front but until then, enjoy the run.

Meditation: *Please help me remember that success is not always what it seems. I realize that getting to the top at someone else's expense will not satisfy me and will make me a target. I will set goals for satisfaction and not status.*

Body:

While sitting, stretch your neck to the left and right then down to your chest and straight back up. Remember, stretching too far back can injure your neck so be careful. All the while you have been doing this exercise you have been strengthening your jawline and erasing little lines in your neck.

When we are losing weight in our arms, stomach, bottom and legs, we forget that we need to tone our neck and face as well. These stretches may be the reason people are asking why you look so rested and healthy.

This exercise also reduces tension headaches.

Money:

Making more money than your neighbor won't make you happier. Having a healthy body and clear conscience will!

Mind:

Study the lives of your heroes. Look at what they started with, the obstacles they overcame, the network they built, and how they ended (or are now). What parallels to your life do they share?

Joke:

Interviewer: "Where would you see yourself in five years?"

Me: "Personally I believe my biggest weakness is in listening."

Day #72

Teach Something Difficult

There is an episode of an old television series in which a documentarian follows the process of the world's last duck flute maker.

A young man becomes fascinated with the ancient, painstaking process from choosing the wood, seasoning the branches to carving the musical instruments, to tuning them. In the end of the episode he asks his subject to teach him how to make the duck-shaped flutes. The old man obliges, making the documentarian the new, last duck flute maker.

I don't know how important duck flutes are to the rest of the world but to that man, who learned his craft from his father, who learned it from his father before him, and who has no sons, they are very important.

We risk losing important parts of our culture if we let intricate crafts like flute-making, Ukrainian egg dying, or wooden bowl lathing die with us. If you have a talent or skill that you believe the world would be worse for losing, please choose someone to pass that skill onto. If there is no one in your family who is interesting in carrying the craft, find a club or organization that promotes a similar activity and let the leaders know you would like to teach a class, or organize one yourself at a local library or community center.

Meditation: *Please help me to realize the importance of heirloom skills. I realize that things that I have been taught still have value in the world. I will learn or try to find someone to wants to learn my unique skill.*

Body:

Your flexibility, endurance and strength have increased. It happened so gradually that you probably didn't know it was happening. The person you were when you started this is slowly becoming the person you envisioned when you bought the book. You have eighteen days to go, just think of much more progress you will have made by then.

Today explore yoga videos online or get one from your library. You still shouldn't do aerobic exercise but beginners yoga is perfect.

Mind:

Write a letter to a teacher or professor that had a positive impact on your life. Recall instances in which you have used the information they gave you, or an anecdote from that time in your life.

Money:

To make extra money, take on students. Math tutors, language tutors and music teachers are in high demand and you can teach them out of your home. The more difficult the subject the more you can charge.

Joke:

What do you get when you wake up on a workday and realize you ran out of coffee?

A depresso.

Day #73

Get Your Hands Dirty

I always pick up discount seeds after planting season and one year my daughter found a pack lying among some batteries in a "junk drawer" in our kitchen.

"Could I still plant these seeds?" she asked with a hopeful look on her face.

"I don't see the harm in trying." I answered although I hated disappointing her with the old packet. Nonetheless we scooped some potting soil into an egg carton and stuck a fingernail sized seed in each egg hole. To my surprise less than a week later the egg carton was full of little plants.

My daughter chose three seedlings to put into her garden. She watered them daily until the soaking spring rains took over. She only had to water them twice during the summer and when autumn came she had nine gorgeous pumpkins to display proudly on our porch. Neighbors wondered where we had found pumpkins with such an unusual color. I couldn't tell them. I hadn't even known they were pumpkin seeds!

I asked her if they were worth the wait and she said. "Those seeds were garbage in a junk drawer but now they are something fun and all we had to do was get a little bit dirty."

There is joy in getting your hands dirty. A little work and a seed can produce results that a trip to the grocery store can never duplicate.

Meditation: *Please help me to experience the joy of growing something from a seed. I understand that nature can give us great things in unexpected packages. I will plant seeds and nurture them to fruition.*

Body:

Stretch before bed each night to relax your body and get nourishing blood flowing to repair the days damage!

If you have a set series of actions you follow each night before you climb between the sheets, you will fall to sleep faster. Studies have shown that when your mind is disciplined by routine, it responds by doing the next logical thing on the list without effort.

Shower, brush your teeth, watch television or read, then lock the doors and turn out the lights to turn off the day and awake refreshed.

Money:

Growing a garden will save money on food, flowers and health bills. Fresh food nourishes cells better than radiated and frozen food and the time you spend weeding and watering is good exercise!

Mind:

Grow an indoor plant. Plants remind us of nature and increase our sense of responsibility. They can make a day indoors more cheerful, as well as clean the carbon dioxide out of the air.

Joke:
What do you call the soft tissue between a shark's teeth?

A slow swimmer.

Day #74

Don't Worry So Much

Worrying increases your risk for cancer and causes heart attacks, high blood pressure and wrinkles. It's a miserable thing to do!

Outside of loss of consciousness, I can't think of a way to instantly quit worrying but I do know simple and effective ways to reduce your worry.

[1]**Do what you can** do to solve it, then release the problem.

[2]**Don't obsess** over things in which you have limited control, the best distraction is to [3]**volunteer, vote, donate and educate** up 10 hours a week. When you are not "on duty" let the world work on the problems. It will.

You are not the only one concerned and you are not the only one working on the problems. [4]**Know that there are others** who share your concerns

[5]**Take a break.** Sometimes you have to [6]**get distance** from things that bother you.

Take a one-week [7]**break from media** and stay away from people who carry bad news. Travel to where the air is clean and no one can find you unless you want them to. You don't have to go far. There are places full of trees within an hour's driving distance of any major city
You can rent a hotel room or pitch a tent for days, weeks or hours.

When you get away from things that worry you, you [8]**see them from a new perspective**. The world won't end without you while you regroup. You will [9]**bring back energy**, new ideas and a little less obsession if you can [10]**fill your mind with happy memories**!

Meditation: *Please help me to clear my mind of thoughts and feelings that get in the way of my happiness and productivity. I realize I can only do so much and that letting go will allow others to do more. I will remove myself from situations that are disturbing my quality of life to refresh myself so that when I return I have more energy to help.*

Body:

With your arms to your sides and your thumbs facing your body push your fist out as far behind you as you comfortable can. Repeat on both side at twenty times. This exercise fights "bat wings" and strengthens the back of your arms and your shoulders. You can add soup cans for more resistance now.

Add weight like soup cans to build strength and fill some of the space where the fat used to be with strong, healthy muscle.

Money:

If you own something high maintenance that is giving you a headache, sell it. No possession is worth sleepless nights.

Mind:

Learn to fix things that break around your house, to change the oil in your car and to garden can save labor costs and the feeling of being able to do something for yourself is worth the effort it takes to learn the skill! (Try YouTube tutorials.)

Joke:
It's been said that women
should not have kids over 40.
40 kids should be enough for anyone.

Day #75

Don't Be Apathetic

It is o.k. to step away for a break, it is not ok to stand by and let everyone else fix your problems.

Mark and his wife Sandy had saved for 15 years to build a house and decided they would hire one contractor instead of a crew and do most of the work themselves. They had plans drawn and chose a contractor who had a reputation for hard, honest work.

The first week went well, all the supplies arrived and the contractor laid them out with written instructions on how the pieces would go together along with measurements and tools at each station. Mark and Sandy chose a station and started to build their house. The contractor had put in a solid foundation so they hammered and cut while he worked at the other end of the house and soon there was a floor.

The second week Mark's back was sore so Sandy and the contractor did most of the heavy lifting. In three days the outer walls were up.

The third week Mark took off to comparison shop for siding and roofing and was often gone all day. Sandy and the contractor stayed to finish the interior walls but without a third man it took twice as long so at the end of the month all that was done was the floor and the skeleton of walls. The rains began.

The roof braces would take a month because Mark was afraid of heights. Another week and the roof plywood was on. It would keep the water from further warping the sub flooring which would now have to be replaced. Another week for shingles and it was starting to look like a house.

"Now that we've got all the heavy work done," Mark declared, (Sandy grimaced at the word "we've".) "You two can run the wiring, you don't need me for that…"

Long story short Sandy left Mark and the shell of a house he didn't want to work on. The project was abandoned like the marriage and today it is a pile of rotting boards.

Meditation: *Please help me to put effort into something I want to accomplish. I realize that I can't expect others to do my own work. I will complete my project by steadily working until it is done.*

Body:

While sitting, stretch your upper body as far to the right and then the left as comfortably possible. Then stretch your arms as high to the ceiling as you can. Repeat twenty times to lengthen and strengthen your waist and back.

Sitting exercises can be done by nearly anyone. If you use a wheelchair, if you're in a hospital bed, or if you are just a couch potato, you can and should do them.

Money:

You can't expect someone else to make money for you even a broker. Being proactive in your wealth building teaches you how to make money. Keep a chart of your income and expenditure sources, update it often.

Mind:

When you are proactive constantly learn how to stay healthy and wealthy. Read at least the headlines of finance and scientific sections of your favorite news site.

Joke:
Meanwhile in a parallel universe: "Oh for God's sake! Where are all these extra single socks coming from?!"

Day #76

Give Someone Another Chance

Maureen saw Ashley, a girl she knew in high school, as she walked past her table on the way out of a restaurant. "Hey, Ashley." She waved.

Ashley looked in her direction, turned back and left.

Later Maureen and Ashley attended the same party.

"There's that bitch Ashley." Maureen sneered. "She's too good to talk to me since she's in college. She won't even say hi."

It was a small house, so eventually the two ran into each other in the kitchen. When Ashley saw Maureen, she said "Hey Maureen, how are you?"
Maureen glared at her and walked on. Ashley was confused. "Hey what's going on?" she followed Maureen.
"You want to talk to me now?" Maureen spit. "But not in front of other people."
"What do you mean?"
"I mean when I saw you last week you didn't want anyone to see you talking to me but in the kitchen it's just fine."
"I have no clue what you are talking about."
"Remember, the Luna Grill, last week, I said 'Hi' to you and you just looked at me and walked out."
"You were there?" Ashley's eyes grew wide. "I didn't see you at all. My husband's ex was in the Luna the last time I was there. She called me out when we were leaving... oh! I guess that was you! I left because I didn't want an argument in a restaurant!"
"I thought you looked right at me. I'm sorry."
"It's o.k. I'm sorry I didn't see you! Hey let's go dance to get people started!"

Maureen and Ashley are still friends because they gave each other another chance. Friends are too valuable to waste, especially good ones. If you give someone a second chance you can heal wounds for two!

Meditation: *Please help me to reconnect with someone I need in my life. I understand it may be difficult to forgive or forget something that happened in the past. I will try to reach someone who has been absent and repair the bond between us.*

Body:

Standing with your legs apart, raise your hands above your head. Bend at the waist and hold your arms perpendicular to your body. Hold for a count of ten, then stand back up straight. Repeat five times, ten if you can. This is a core strengthening exercise that burns fat in your arms as well.

Money:

Get important information in writing so there will be no misunderstanding later. You can use it for evidence if you ever have to go to court.

Mind:

Writing in a diary relieves stress, strengthens fine motor and estimation skills. Also, it's a fun way to see what you were doing a year or ten years ago!

Joke:
My son did surprisingly well on his driver's test yesterday. He got 8 out of 12.
The other 4 managed to jump out of the way.

Day #77

Be a Good Citizen

In a European fairy tale, there was a rock so big in the middle of the road that carriages had to go around it to continue their journey. The detour was cutting deep grooves into the road when it was wet that turned to wheel breaking bumps when it was dry.

A woman in one carriage endured the bumpy ride across the dried-out grooves and called to her driver, "Remind me to write a letter to the king!"

A man on a horse yelled to another who was passing, "Someone should do something about that rock in the road, it's dangerous."

"I agree, we should contact the King about it!" called the other man.

A traveler who had been resting under a tree overheard the ruckus. He looked around for help and finding no one willing to help, he used his walking stick as a lever to pry the rock from the mud and roll it to the side of the road. When he went back to fill in the hole he saw that, where the rock had been, was a small metal box which he opened. Inside he found three gold pieces and a letter that read. "If you are reading this you have moved the rock from the road. Please come to the castle for your reward."

The young man started his life in the community a very rich man but he never stopped doing good deeds when he recognized a need for them.

Meditation: *Please help me to recognize a need that I can fill. I realize that I shouldn't ask my government to do simple things I can do myself. I will perform simple tasks instead of complaining that no one does anything about problems.*

Body:

Week eleven, less than 2 weeks to go!
Weigh yourself. Measure your neck, chest, arms, waist, legs, and hips. Take pictures, blog and/or update the chart! Have you come as far you thought you would? Are you surprised that you have surpassed it?
Now is the time to start *looking for a gym*. Find one that is not too crowded, has adequate parking and is open when you need it. A lot of gyms offer a one-week trial membership. Take this advantage to see which one is for you.

Money:

Doing favors for others can also benefit you. Fixing a broken slat in your neighbor's fence will keep his dog from digging up your roses!

Mind:

Repeat what you want to remember or write it down. Pulling a name or a grocery list out of the visual and into the audio or tactile memory or vice versa cements it in your mind.

Joke:
Dentist: "Looks like you need a crown."
My daughter: "Finally someone understands me"

Day #78

Schedule Good Deeds

A librarian told the man in front of the line that he had overdue book fines and would not be able to check anything out until they were paid. He pulled out his debit card and the librarian said her terminal was down and she couldn't accept plastic. He rummaged in his pockets but still came up short. The woman behind him fumbled in her purse and laid some money on the counter, "Will this cover it?"

The man started to protest but the woman cut him off. "I promised my Girl Scout troop I would do a good deed every week. I have not done my good deed for this week and tonight is our meeting! You just solved my problem by letting me solve yours!" she beamed. The librarian took the money and smiled at the man and the woman. Both checked out their books and the man thanked the scout leader with a promise that he would do a good deed too.

I like the idea of scheduling good deeds. Perhaps we should all do a weekly good deed for someone. Pick up groceries for an elderly or injured friend. Read to someone in a care center or hospital. Rake someone's leaves. Pay someone's turnpike toll. Just one good deed a week, 52 good deeds a year, will make a huge difference, of course you can add more if you like!

Meditation: *Please help me remember to do good deeds without expecting payment on a regular basis. I realize that being active in a positive way builds a good reputation for me and spreads good feelings among others. I will mark on my calendar three good deeds that I will do before the end of this program.*

Body:

Stand with your legs apart at shoulder width, then bend your legs and lower your body at least 6 inches, then stand. Do it 10 times as fast as you can, then rest.

Repeat three to five times, this is thigh buster that your body should be ready for after all the walking you have done. Add this to your favorite exercises three times a week.

Money:

Schedule automatic payments through your bank account or utility companies to avoid late fees and collection charges.

Mind:

A daily *and* a monthly calendar will keep you on top of chores and obligations. Put it somewhere you often look for best results. (bathroom door, refrigerator)

Joke:
If you forget to pay for exorcism,
will you get repossessed?

Day #79

Take the Scenic Route

We had been on the highway for four hours and it was time for a break. While everyone was using the facilities and picking up snacks, I looked over the map. (Yes, these were pre-historic times.) I'm not fond of highways and prefer to take the back road if one is available. I found a route that would cut about an hour off our time (if the traffic wasn't bad) and talked the group into allowing me to take the detour.

Fifteen minutes into the drive one of the children let out a loud screech! I braked and pulled over to the side of the road thinking it must be a spider. She was squealing incoherently as I parked the car to calm her down. I heard a low, loud "Shooooosh" above the car. I looked up and there, just above us was a gorgeous, gigantic, hot air balloon! It was so close we could hear the conversation of the people in the basket!

We sat there on the hood of the car on that the hill as twenty-three more glided over at different altitudes. The kids jumped around in fascination and yelled "Hello!" to the ballooners who spoke to them as we counted and picked our favorites.

Had we taken the highway we would have quickly passed the beautiful balloons. Because of our detour we have a good memory we can draw on when we need a happy thought.

Meditation: *Please help me choose another route occasionally to expand my knowledge of my country and experience new things. I understand that the best things in life can be found in unusual places. I will find an alternate route to places I visit and look for treasure.*

Body:

While standing facing a wall, stretch one leg out as far behind you as you comfortably can. Relax. Repeat on both legs at least twenty times. You should feel some resistance after yesterdays speed squats.

Notice that although you are working a different part of your leg, the two sets of muscles rely on each other. When you isolate a part of your body you strengthen it to support others.

Money:

Find a short cut and a long cut to work, listen to the radio and check your phone as you get ready for work. If there is a road delay you will be able to stay on schedule even if your phone is dead.

Mind:

When you allow time for improvisation you leave space for good things to happen. Leave early and expect to get there later for a relaxing trip. Peace of mind makes up for "lost" time.

Joke:
Where do you bring horses that are sick?
To the horsepital.

Day #80

Turn Off your Television

According to recent statistics most Americans watch between 4 and 8 hours of television a day, including internet videos. That is 6 hours a day they will never get back. Six hours to watch someone else's fictional life instead of experiencing their own real one.

Watching for four hours and using the other two to do homework or study would produce better grades that might lead to scholarships or entrance into a great college!

Watching for 3 hours and using the other 3 swimming and exercising or bicycling in a park would lead to healthier children and adults with stronger bodies who have more confidence and look great!

Television has been called a vast wasteland because nothing grows in it, definitely not your mind. It wastes time and its advertisements cause you to spend money on things you really neither want nor need. Your self-esteem also suffers as you see people living glamorous artificial lives that make your life look pathetic by comparison. (Believe me: the people in those shows lead boring lives off screen as well!)

Try to go without tv for a week but be sure to stock up on great books, and healthy activity plans beforehand. (and educational videos for if you just can't do it). Like a day without electricity it will be an experience you will remember for years to come.

Meditation: *Please help me to try to live without television more often. I realize I can get information from more reliable sources. I will spend less time watching television and more time building a healthy life for myself and my family.*

Body:

Day eighty is a good time to do the conscious relaxation exercise. Remember? Tighten first your face then release it, then your neck and chest, then arms and hands, then stomach, then bottom, then legs and feet. It's great for body awareness too!

Money:

With basic cable at $39.99 a month you will pay over $500 a year including taxes and fees. (More with late charges and pay per view) Many television shows can now be seen online for free.

Mind:

Make a list of things you can accomplish in an hour. Instead of watching a show you don't like much, choose a task and get started!

Joke:
What do you call a totally unimportant elephant?
An Irrelephant.

Day #81

Listen to Music

Judy won four free tickets to see Neil Zaza, a celebrated guitarist, play a Christmas show at a fancy theater. She took her son and her son's best friend.

She wasn't a fan of hard rock music, but the boys were really looking forward to the show and their excitement was contagious.

The curtain rose and the next two hours were an exciting and eclectic mix of new Christmas songs and carols from her childhood, interpreted in ways she had never dreamed possible. Everyone left the show overwhelmed by the talent of the musicians and the professionalism of the show and Judy opened her mind to appreciate a new kind of music.

Live music is an experience that everyone should have. The formulaic songs on the radio are noise compared to good music played by real musicians.
Free live music is available in churches, schools, colleges, and in the summer, in bigger city park districts.

Music is powerful. Psychologists have proven that people can be convinced to hurry up, slow down, buy more, and even buy certain products when exposed to different songs in a consumer atmosphere.

Animals exposed to soothing music are calmed by it, and babies exposed to several styles of music learn to speak sooner and with more varied inflection than infants who are exposed to silence.

Meditation: *Please help me to include music in my life and to seek out live music when it is available. Exposure to different types of music will improve my mind and my social skills. I will experiment with new music.*

Body:

Remember the "bicycle? Lie on your back and lift your legs in the air perpendicular to your hips. Put your hands behind your head for support and slowly do a bicycle motion in the air for a full minute. For a more challenging workout, try to lift your bottom off of the mat as you do the bicycle motion.

Doing this exercise to music makes you want to do it longer and you'll achieve better results.

Money:

Use the library for CDs or the internet to listen to different types of music without purchasing it. When you find something you love, please buy it! (The artist also gets credit through the library's reporting system.)

Mind:

Sing along to songs if you know the lyrics. You don't have to be loud enough for anyone to hear, but sing. Music inhabits a deep part of our brains and even patients with Alzheimer's can sometimes remember lyrics from their youth. How many songs do you know "by heart"?

Bad Joke:
What did the cowboy say to the cow on the barn roof?
Get down, cow!

Day #82

Make Music

Did you know that humming stimulates the brain and can help you think faster? Did you know toe tapping burns 9 calories an hour? Did you know singing along with songs on the radio improves your vocal range?

Toe tapping, humming, singing along to a song are all ways for non-trained musicians to make music.

Music is such a part of our collective psyches that in some cultures, songs are used as courtship rituals. The best singer attracts the best mates! (Anyone who has seen a pop music concert can understand this!)

Making music is nearly as important as listening to music. Kids who learn to play music score better on math tests, memorize educational material faster, interact with others more easily and have more self-confidence.

It's never too late to learn. Some instant instruments to learn include bongo drums, maracas, tambourine, egg shakers and kazoo. Anyone with rhythm can make *some* kind of music. (Good music takes practice.)

Easy instruments that take a minimum of instruction include harmonica, ocarina, tin whistle, and xylophone.

Once you've mastered rudimentary instruments move up to something more difficult. Playing music is a great way to use your time. People are drawn to musicians so it is also a good way to meet new friends!

Meditation: *Please help me remember to experiment with an instrument or to make music with objects around me. I realize that music is part of the human psyche and can be an excellent way to express myself. I will at least hum along with a song today.*

Body:

Lie on your back and with your arms to your side raise first one leg then the other slowly straight up to the ceiling and back down. Bend your knees and put your feet on the floor. Lift your butt off the floor and hold for a count of five, Repeat ten times. Raise both legs together for a tighter belly!

Money:

Most music stores rent instruments and equipment. If you find you are good at something, and want to continue, they sometimes apply part of the rent toward the purchase price.

Mind:

If you find you aren't good at string instruments try woodwinds, if you don't like that, try percussion etc. until you find a way to express your musical soul with the instrument of your choice even if it's your own voice!

Joke:
What is blue and smells like red paint?
Blue paint.

Day #83

Appreciate Art

From caveman paintings of mammoths to Andy Warhol's paintings of groceries, art has been a way for humans to express what is important in a society.

Visual art enriches your thoughts. Colors, textures, and shades of light and dark fill your mind with images of times past, different perspectives of what you see today and possibilities for the future.

To embrace art is to embrace life.

If it's been a while since you've visited a museum or if you have never been to one you are missing something rare and enriching. If you can, go alone to experience the masterpieces at your own pace. Alone, you have the freedom to take your time and look closely. What you want to look at, a friend might not want to see.

If you must go with others take along a piece of paper and a pen. Along the way, write down the names of artists to which you are drawn. You can then find books of their art or study them online. When you find time to visit the gallery or museum again, you can look for more of that artist's pieces.

Art galleries as opposed to museums are businesses and the art on the walls is for sale. Museums rarely sell the pieces on display. Many museums sell posters of the art in their permanent collections so if you see something you like, you can browse the gift shop for a print to frame for your own collection.

Meditation: *Please help me to look at works of art with an eye toward what I like. I realize that what I'm most attracted to will satisfy, calm or invigorate me. I will visit an art gallery or museum in my area as soon as possible.*

Body:

While standing, hold your arms straight out to your sides, keeping your arms straight raise your arms and bring your hands together above your head, lower them to your sides and press against your hips. Repeat ten to twenty times.

This exercise strengthens and tones upper arms. To add more calorie burning power, add a squat to each repetition.

Money:

Many museums have free admission days or reduced-price admission on special days. All of the museums of the Smithsonian are free.
(Our taxes pay for them.)

Mind:

Look for hidden meaning in the titles of works you don't understand. Modern art often expresses an emotion rather than an item. Experiment with naming the works yourself!

Joke:
If I were to choose between dating
and eating soup, I think I'd eat the soup.
Not much point in dating it.

Day #84

Make Art

When you were a kid you may have made macaroni bracelets for Mother's Day or painted with a plastic multipack of water colors. Your art was proudly displayed until your mother felt it was appropriate to put it away or until you made another piece to take its place. But did you ever make a piece that she kept after she took it down from the refrigerator or a piece so good you just couldn't wait to get it home?

Sometimes, either by accident or talent we put together something that tells how we feel or think or want to be.

That is art.

To neglect the creative side of ourselves is to stifle a genius of expression. Even if your art teacher told you to "step away from the crayons before you hurt someone" you must not give up.

Use your creative side to doodle on notes, decorate cookies with a child, mold your hair into a cone shape in the shower, or drawn stick figures in the sand at the beach. Drawing, painting, arranging objects, and forming 3 dimensional shapes awakens areas of our brains that allow us to solve problems and create new ideas.

Maybe, like Anna Mary Robinson, (aka Grandma Moses) you will discover your artistic ability late in life or use it to open your brain to more creative thought.

Meditation: *Please help me to use my thoughts and feeling to make "art" of my own. I understand that by attempting to create something that captures my feelings I am opening my mind to new ideas. I will take a few minutes out of my day to attempt a creative project.*

Body

Week 12! The Homestretch!

You know the drill. Weigh yourself. Measure your neck, chest, arms, waist, legs and hips. Deep condition your hair, mask your face, paint your nails. Take pictures, blog and/or update the chart!

Stretching and isometrics should be a daily habit for you by now. The exercises you have learned have been repeated enough times for you to know how to use them when your body feels stiff or needs more energy. Try to combine some of them into a comfortable routine you can make as much a habit as walking.

Money:

You can make 3D art with shredded newspapers, black and white art with pencils, colored art with a child's crayons or watercolors to get started. No investment is needed until you find your talent!

Mind:

Try drawing or painting with your non-dominant hand (left if you are a righty, right if you are a lefty) to awaken centers in your brain that will give you new ideas and help you solve more difficult problems.

Joke:

Apparently taking a day off is not something you should do when you work for a calendar company.

Day #85

Give to Be an Example

Have you ever noticed that when a tip-jar on a counter is empty it tends to stay that way? As soon as someone puts a dollar into it, someone else will do the same. If someone drops in coins someone else will drop in coins as well. Someone must start the giving.

My favorite way to begin the chain is to ask several people what they think someone needs for a new baby, apartment or dorm room. I will sometimes tell people what I'm thinking of getting to help them think of ideas themselves.

I hate office collections. When someone is collecting for a baby shower or wedding I ask for the bride/groom or parent's name and location so I can give a gift that I have chosen. Five or ten dollars is easy to give but it often goes toward a plastic trinket or flowers that the person tosses on their way out of the building.

When I send the gift to the person I sometimes add a note to the card, "Please forgive my not donating at the office collection taken by "Jane Doe". I saw that she was doing well enough without me and wanted you to know I was thinking of you too." A bonus message this sends is: There was a collection taken in your name, if you didn't get the gift, this is the person to see. (Keeps sketchy people honest.)

Starting the giving is also a good idea for things like, second wedding, late age "surprise" babies, retirements, adoptions and house fires.

Meditation: *Please help me to lead the way when I see someone in need. I will see to it that my gift is thoughtful and timely. If I see that no one is organizing an effort to help someone in need, I will.*

Body

On your hands and knees, lift one leg up to the height of your bottom (no further) slowly lower it and repeat ten to twenty times per leg.

You can add leg weights if this has become too easy or if you want to build muscle in the backs of your legs.

Money:

If you don't know or associate with someone in your office for whom a collection is being taken you are under no obligation to give.

Mind:

Find a funny comic and post in your work area that illustrates your distaste for office collections or pools. If you are nervous about saying no to an office beggar, just point to it!

Joke:
An astronaut and a rhinoceros are knitting on the beach, a Rubik's cube rolls up to them, then flies away.
"That's madness!" the Rhino said.
"Yes." said the astronaut. "He could have said hello."

Day #86

Keep a Tiny Treasure

When my grandmother died, we cleaned her house and on a little end table, beside where she always sat I found a tiny plastic squirrel that was worn to nearly unrecognizable. I asked one of my cousins what it was and she said, "Gram said that little squirrel used to remind her to save for harder times...you know like a squirrel does for winter."

I put that little squirrel in my purse and carried it for three years. Every time I saw it I was reminded not only to save money, but of my dear sweet grandma who always had enough of everything to give some away.

A tiny treasure can be anything from a lucky bus token to a rubber frog your child gave you for Christmas. The object itself doesn't matter; its meaning is paramount.

Look in your jewelry box or trinket tray. Chances are you already own a tiny treasure. What is the memory or gift it has for you? Do you have a fifty-cent piece from your uncle or granddad? What was it about him you loved so much that you kept the coin? That's the true treasure.

If you don't already have one, a good small treasure is a charm that reminds you of your goal. If you want to be a famous musician carry a tiny guitar, if your goal is to run the New York Marathon carry a little shoe.

Kept in your pocket, your tiny talisman will help you keep your mind on your goal or on someone you admire and want to emulate.

Meditation: *Please help me to choose a small treasure that means enough to keep it with me. I know that it will be a reminder of who I am and where I'm going. I will look for a little gift to carry with me today.*

Body

Now that you have been exercising regularly and your body feels comfortable with increased activity, you might want to try new things. Tai Chi is a wonderful exercise for control and breathing. Its measured moves feel like dance and look like karate. Go online and look for free Tai Chi beginners' videos or enroll at a gym that offers classes.
Just give it a try.

Money:

A coin your grandfather gave you might be worth a lot of money but is the sentimental value worth more than the money? If you need the money badly ask someone to take a photo of you holding it. The photo will keep the memory for you.

Mind:

We use our hands to create memories and associations in our minds just as we do with smells, tastes, sounds and sights. If you want someone to remember something, hold their hand while you tell them. If you want to remember something, write it.

Joke:
What do you call an alligator wearing a vest?
An investigator.

Day #87

Express Kindness

I knew it was a wrong number as soon as I heard the old voice. Since my grandmother died I don't know anyone over the age of 70.

"I'm trying to get in touch with someone my son knew, Deborah Howard, and I was wondering if you are her."

I am listed as D. Howard, low on the list among many in my area so I knew she had called several other people.

"I'm not, but I may be able to help you." I offered. "Can you tell me a little about her?"
The little voice sounded relieved. "Well, she would be about fifty-seven and she used to live in Akron.

I was already at my computer so I opened a database that I subscribed to. "Let's see, what was her maiden name?

"Sellers." she said it quickly and said it again. "Her name is Deborah Howard now."

I typed in the information and there she was, two down from the top: Formerly Deborah Sellers of Akron, Ohio she now went as Deborah Mitchell of Santa Fe, New Mexico. She worked as a paralegal and had two speeding tickets in the past ten years.

"Would you believe she's in New Mexico now?" I asked.
"Is that a fact? She said. "Do you know her number?"
It was right in front of me and I recited it slowly so she could take down the information. "Got it?"
"Yes, and I thank you so much dear, you see my son died and she was on a list of people he wanted me to contact." Her voice was steady, I had the feeling her son had suffered as she was dealing well with his passing. "She was the only one I couldn't find."

A week later I got another call. The woman sounded twenty years younger. "I wanted to thank you for helping me find Deborah Howard. She came to the service and do you know who she brought with her? Her son who she tells me is my grandson! He looks just like his dad! I can't thank you enough!"

Meditation: *Please help me to extend kindness to strangers even when they don't ask. I realize that the little bit of good I can do may make a big difference to someone else. I will offer to help someone today.*

Body

You don't need a stair-stepper machine to work on your thighs and bottom. Use your staircase at home or go to a nearby place that has stairs. You will find them in parks, at libraries and in court houses. Some people have even been known to walk "up" a "down" escalator (during times when no one is using it, of course).

Money:

Buy free trade coffee, tea and local produce when you can. The little bit of money will be worth it in the peace of mind you get from knowing no one suffered for your breakfast.

Mind:

If you're learning something tough but important, read and repeat it once an hour for an entire day.

Joke:

Two years ago, I asked the girl of my dreams on a date, today I asked her to marry me.

She said no, on both occasions.

Day #88

Express Appreciation

Thank you notes, those little things your mother made you send when you were a kid, can open doors for you!

There is an old story about lady Diana of how the shy gawky girl became famous by reaching out to those around her with thank you notes. She thanked waiters, parents of the children she taught, people she met at parties, and of course those who gave her gifts. Those people became her cheerleaders and advocates until her death in 1997. She is one of the world's most beloved and well-recognized people.

When you say, "Thank you." with a note, you are giving a token of gratitude and recognition. When you neglect a note, you seem aloof and uncaring.

Thank you notes should be written and sent promptly. Many times I've written a thank you note and put it on a pile of papers meaning to send it, only to find it several months later, too late. (I send it anyway.)

Thank you notes should not be procrastinated. Like Christmas cards, there is a deadline. If someone has not received a card or call within two weeks of a gift or service they may assume you didn't receive it and call to inquire or they may think perhaps incorrectly that their gift meant little to you and move on from there.

A prompt, heartfelt thank you will go a long way toward building your reputation as a kind, giving person who is worthy of further attention. Thank someone with a card or letter today!

Meditation: *Please help me to express gratitude for gifts I have received. I know that saying thank you is a fundamental courtesy that should be done in writing when possible. I will write a thank you letter today.*

Body

The healthy effect of deep breathing cannot be emphasized enough. Strong lungs make it easier to run, swim, or do anything that requires endurance. Before getting out of bed take ten very deep breaths, breathing a five count in and a five count out.
When you rise, you'll have more energy!

Money:

Write thank you notes to companies whose products you appreciate and they will sometimes send coupons for free items!

Mind:

Remember to be grateful when you learn a lesson, good or bad. Keeping an attitude of graciousness will earn you a reputation as a wise person.

Joke:
It's not a fine restaurant when you tell the water to take his thumb off of your steak and he says, "And let it fall on the floor again?"

Day #89

Accept Praise and Appreciation

Accepting praise and gratitude is an area in which more people could use a lesson in poise.

Joey had no formal training but he was always taking cars apart and putting them back together and when someone he knew had a breakdown he was usually able to get the car running again.

One Sunday afternoon Junior, an old man who lived three doors down from Joey couldn't get his car to start. Joey pulled his car up to Junior's and connected the jumper cables. No matter how long they charged the battery they couldn't get the car to start. Joey disconnected the cables and said "I'll be right back." He went home and came back with a solenoid. He put the solenoid in Junior's car and the car started right up!

Thank you, Joe. You're a good man!" Junior said and he patted Joey on his back. "Wasn't much." Joey said as he threw the jumper cables in his car.

Later that night Junior's wife had a heart issue and he used the car to rush her to the hospital.

Junior told neighbors about the day and called Joey a hero. Joey looked embarrassed by the compliment.

"Dammit Joe, you saved my wife's life! The old man bellowed and coughed. When Joey saw how worked up it made Junior to have to work so hard to give him a compliment he grinned and said, "Thank you."

The two were very good friends to the end of Junior's life and when he died he left the car to Joe.

Meditation: *Please help me to accept praise with grace. I realize it's a compliment and I'm grateful for the recognition. I will say "thank you" when praised.*

Body

Do you have time and energy for more exercise? If so design your own routine. Make a weekly schedule. Be sure to include exercises that tone all of your body! Think about the parts of your body that might still wiggle, think about parts that might need more strength and concentrate more heavily on those areas.

Money:

When you get a thank you note, no reply is necessary but a short receipt confirmation call will win loyalty. It is an easy way to build a following that can help you when you ask for a raise or promotion.

Mind:

When someone says, "Thank you." try to say, "You're Welcome."
Saying "No probs.' or "Ain't no thing." can mark you as immature.

Joke:
An alleged billionaire hired a lawyer who reassured him: "You'll never go to jail with that kind of money."
The lawyer was right. When the man went to jail, he didn't have a penny left."

Day #90

Never Stop Learning

Edie was 56 when she first stepped onto a campus. She had always wanted to be a lawyer and after many years as an assistant to one she finally decided to follow her dreams.

For four years on her way to classes she heard comments like, "What do you teach?" and "Excuse me professor, could you guide me to..." and for three more she heard, "I'm sorry Ma'am this mock trial is for enrolled students only." and "Are you looking for a law student for legal aid?"

Finally, at the age of 63 she earned her Jurus Doctorate and started working for the law firm for whom she had been an underpaid assistant. It was months before some of the older partners stopped giving her papers to type but now she is a proud partner herself.

Alex was a 16-year-old technology wizard when he had to leave high school for health reasons. He took the G.E.D. and although he had the highest score in his county he found that because of his age, no local company would hire him even though he knew more about networking and software than many programmers and technicians. He found a college that would allow him to take classes on Tuesdays and Thursdays and discovered his true passion in biology. He is working toward a medical degree with plans to research and find a cure for the disease that cut short his high school career.

It's never too early or too late to finish school. The world benefits from educated people and educated people benefit from the continued exposure to new information.

Meditation: *Please help me to keep my mind sharp by learning every day just for the information. I will strive to learn something that I have been lacking and use my knowledge to improve my life and the lives of others.*

Body:

Congratulations. You did it! You've been eating a low-calorie plant-based diet for twelve weeks.

Use what you have learned to keep weight off or take off a few pounds if they start to invade again! This is your go-to way of eating now, but you can splurge on occasion.

For the final time, weigh yourself, measure your neck, chest, arms, waist, legs and hips. Look at that chart. You might want to have a party to celebrate the end of the program and to show off your progress! THIS is a reason to celebrate.

Mind:

Organize a specific place for things you use every day (keys, glasses, calendar, shopping list) to avoid wasting time and energy looking for them.

Money:

Invest in your education and the education of your children. It is the single most important thing you can do with your money.

Joke:
"Mom, don't get alarmed, but I'm at the hospital."
"Son, please. You've been a surgeon for 8 years now. Can you just say, "Hello, mom."?

Suggestions and Recipes

Breakfast

1. A glass of ice water followed by a bowl of chopped apples, bananas and blueberries.

2. A glass of ice water followed by 2 peaches, nectarine or one can of peaches in water, not syrup.

3. A glass of ice water followed by a sliced apple and a small orange.

4. A glass of ice water followed by one large grapefruit or a medium orange.

5. A glass of ice water followed by a fruit smoothie made with ½ cup berries, ½ of a banana, 2 leaves of lettuce and ½ cup orange juice or water. (Add a peach or some crushed pineapple if you like.)

6. A glass of ice water followed by half a medium cantaloupe with optional berries.

7. A glass of ice water followed by a fruit salad made with pineapple, banana, and mandarin oranges.

8. A glass of water followed by two cups of chopped fruit. (Cantaloupe, strawberries, apples, blueberries.)

9. A glass of ice water followed by a salt-free vegetable bouillon sauté of chopped zucchini or crookneck squash, chopped green or red pepper and onion and mushrooms. If you need it, use a salt substitute like Mrs. Dash.

10. A glass of ice water followed by a smoothie of mixed frozen fruit, spirulina and water.

11. A glass of ice water followed by a mango, papaya or banana.

Lunch Salads

Hollowed Tomato Salad Finely chopped romaine lettuce, celery, cooked and cooled quinoa and chopped avocado inside a hollowed tomato.

Sweet Bean Salad ½ cup black beans on a generous bed of chopped lettuce, topped with a dressing made by blending ¼ cup chopped red pepper, ½ cup chopped zucchini, 2 tablespoons lime juice, 4 tablespoons brewer's yeast, 1 tsp raisins, and a dash of cayenne pepper.

Avocado Garden Salad A bed of lettuce with chopped avocado and chopped red onions with a dressing of 1/3 cup fresh orange juice, 1 tsp apple cider vinegar, 2 tbsp sesame seeds, ½ tsp powdered ginger, and 1 tsp raisins blended until smooth.

Berry Salad. A bed of lettuce topped with strawberries, blueberries or raspberries, chopped walnuts or pecans and a dressing made by blending 1 cup strawberries, ½ an orange, a teaspoon of raisins and a splash of apple cider vinegar.

Pineapple Salad. A lettuce salad topped with chopped pineapple, sautéed in a non-stick pan with a large dollop of cranberry sauce topped with a sprinkle of walnuts.

Southwest Lettuce Wraps. Two lettuce leaves wrapped around a pulsed mixture of ½ cup each carrot, walnuts, tomato, onion, and ½ teaspoon each of cumin, garlic powder, and chili powder.

Fruit Salad Chopped apples, raisins, berries, and cantaloupe tossed with ¼ cup orange juice.

California Wrap Well chopped lettuce, tomato and onion in a lettuce leaf with avocado, chopped almonds and a dollop of salsa.

Black Bean and Quinoa Salad Chopped tomatoes, avocado, onions, and red peppers ½ cup red beans and ½ cup cooked quinoa, tossed with a dressing made by blending ¼ cup chopped red pepper, ½ cup chopped zucchini, 2 tablespoons lime juice, 4 tablespoons brewer's yeast, 1 tablespoon raisins, and a dash of cayenne pepper.

Taco Salad A bed of lettuce with chopped tomatoes and jalapenos, topped with unsalted baked tortilla chips and a dollop of salsa.

Tropical Salad Chopped bananas, oranges, pineapples, and cooked quinoa topped by a dressing made by blending 1 cup chopped mango, ½ an orange, a teaspoon of raisins and a splash of apple juice.

Lunch Soups

Veggie Stew

2 medium onions
5 cloves minced garlic
8 sliced mushrooms
5 chopped celery stalks
4 thinly sliced carrots
1 small head of chopped cabbage
2 quarts water
1 large can diced tomatoes
1 tablespoon Mrs. Dash Spicy
3 tablespoons vegetable flavored bouillon.

Sauté all vegetables in a non-stick pan with a little water until soft. Add water, tomatoes, spice and bouillon. Simmer until celery and carrots are soft, serve hot.

Summer Squash Soup

1 whole onion
2 whole heads garlic
2 diced yellow squash unpeeled
OR 1 large seeded zucchini halved lengthwise
1 medium potato washed but unpeeled
1 qt water
1 tablespoon vegetable flavor bouillon
½ tsp Mrs. Dash spicy
1 cup unsweetened coconut milk

Cut the ends off the onion, garlic, squash and potato and roast for 45 minutes or until soft.
Pulse in food processor while hot with water, bouillon, spices and coconut milk. Serve warm.

Winter Veggie Soup

To large soup pot add:
1/2 cup red lentils
1 qt. water
½ head cauliflower florets
2 chopped bell peppers
1 can diced carrots
1 can diced tomatoes
1 can kidney beans
1 can pumpkin
1 chopped onion
1 tsp garlic powder
2 tbsp vegetable flavor bouillon
3 cups chopped kale
Simmer for 30 minutes. Serve hot.

Corn Chowder

Into crock pot place:
1 ½ quarts water
2 cans low sodium corn
4 cups diced potatoes
1 chopped onion
1 tsp garlic powder
1 can diced carrots
1 chopped stalk of celery
2 cups coconut milk
2 tbsp lime juice or 1 tbsp lemon juice
1 tsp Mrs. Dash spicy

Cook overnight on low. Serve hot.

Can't Be Vegan Chili

Into a crock pot place:

- 1 can diced carrots
- 2 cans kidney beans
- 1 large can diced tomatoes
- 1 can tomato paste
- 1 can unsalted corn
- 2 cans water
- 3 stalks chopped celery
- 1 chopped green pepper
- 1 tablespoon garlic
- 1 chopped onion
- 1 cup quinoa
- 2 tbsp cumin
- 1 tbsp paprika
- 1 chili powder
- 2 tbsp soy sauce
- 2 tsp Sriracha

Cook overnight on low. Serve hot.

Red Lentil Soup

Into a crockpot place:

- 3 cups red lentils
- 1 quart water
- 1 can diced carrots
- 1 can diced tomatoes
- 1 can peas
- 1 diced potato
- 2 chopped onions
- 4 minced garlic cloves
- ½ tsp ginger powder
- 1 tbps cumin
- 1 tbsp curry powder
- 2 tbsp vegetable flavor bouillon

Cook overnight on low. Serve hot.

Fasolada

Into a soup pot place:

- 2 qts. water
- 1 tsp garlic powder
- 1 chopped onion
- 4 stalks chopped celery
- 1 can diced carrots
- 1 can of tomatoes
- 2 cans white beans
- 2 tsp. thyme
- 1 bay leaf
- 2 tbsp lime juice
- 2 tbsp no-salt vegetable bouillon
- 1 tsp. Mrs. Dash spicy

Add water onion, celery to a soup pot and bring to a rolling boil, add remaining ingredients and lower to simmer for 30-40 minutes. Remove bay leaf. Serve hot.

Chickpea Curry Soup

Into a soup pot add:
- 1 chopped onion
- 1 teaspoon minced garlic
- 1 can diced carrots
- 1 can diced tomatoes
- 1 can pumpkin
- 1 can chickpeas
- 1 tbsp curry
- 1/2 tsp ginger
- ½ tsp Mrs. Dash spicy
- 1 can coconut milk
- 1 cup water
- 1/2 lime

Simmer 20-30 minutes. Serve hot over quinoa.

Tomato Bisque

1 cup chopped onion
1 can diced carrots
1 tbsp minced garlic
2 cans tomato
2 cups water
1 tbsp no-salt vegetable bouillon
1 tsp Mrs. Dash (regular, not spicy)
½ tsp basil
1 tsp honey
1/4 cup cashews

Cook onions and garlic in 1 cup water until soft. Add remaining ingredients and blend until smooth. Return to pot and simmer 15 minutes. Serve hot.

Quick Easy Broccoli Soup

1 can coconut milk
1 head of broccoli florets (no stems)

Cook broccoli in coconut milk until soft. Blend, serve hot.

Green Earth Pho

- 1 tsp ginger powder
- 1 chopped onion
- 1 bag dried shitakes
- 2 tbsp minced garlic
- 1 chopped lemongrass stalk
- ½ tsp cinnamon
- ¼ cup chopped fennel
- 4 chopped scallions
- ½ cup soy sauce
- 4 cups water
- 1 qt water
- 2 tbsp vegetable flavor bouillon
- 1 pack cooked brown rice noodles

Toppings: Bean sprouts, tofu cubes, lime juice, fresh basil, chopped broccoli, mushrooms, bok choy, chopped cilantro, scallions

Caramelize onions in a non-stick pan with a tsp water. Add everything but noodles and toppings. Simmer for 30-45 minutes.

Strain through cheesecloth. Toss out spent vegetables and spices, add noodles to broth, serve with toppings.

Dinner

Spaghetti Squash

Cut one spaghetti squash in half lengthwise, remove seeds and place flat side down on a baking sheet. Bake 40 minutes or until soft. Scoop out strings and top with sauce as you would spaghetti.
(Alternative: Spiralize zucchini to make spaghetti, dip in boiling water before serving to soften.)
Some good sauces include:

Tomato Sauce

1 can tomato sauce	¼ tsp oregano
1 roasted onion	¼ tsp basil
1 roaster peppers	Mrs. Dash to taste

Red Pepper Sauce

1 jar roasted red peppers	1 tsp. vinegar
1 can artichoke hearts	1 clove garlic
½ cup fresh basil	1 tsp oregano
	2 tbs cashews

Blend, enjoy. Refrigerate and use within a week.

Avocado Dressing

1 avocado	½ cup water
1 tbsp lime juice	1 tbsp cilantro
½ cucumber	½ tsp chili powder

Blend, enjoy immediately.
Delicious on salads as well (add ½ tsp vinegar).

"Cheezle" (Cheesy drizzle)
1 tbsp ground chia seeds
3 tbsp water
1 peeled zucchini blotted dry
3 tbsp red pepper
1 tbsp lime juice
4 tbsp brewer's yeast
1 tbsp raisins
1 tbsp ground chia seeds
1 tbsp chopped cashews
1/4 tsp chili powder (optional)
Blend, refrigerate ½ hour to "gel" and then use on spaghetti squash, quinoa, taco salad, Enchilada Casserole or Buffalo Cauliflower (all below).

Stir Fry

Pour ¼ cup vegetable broth in the bottom of a hot wok then while stirring add your choice of:

Green/red peppers	Peanuts (a few!)
Sliced onions	Asparagus
Sliced mushrooms	Zucchini
Sliced Carrots	Scallions
Broccoli	Sliced garlic
Cauliflower	Pea pods
Bean sprouts	Bok choy
Bamboo shoots	Baby corn

Quickly* toss with 3 tbsp soy sauce, grated ginger and 1 tbsp maple syrup until vegetables are softer but still crisp, Serve over zucchini noodles or brown rice.
*If you let it sit without tossing it will steam then burn rather than sautéing.

Buffalo Cauliflower
Chop cauliflower into florets and toss to coat in Louisiana hot sauce bake until soft and dry. Serve with "Cheezle" and celery stalks or with chopped avocado and prepared brown rice.

Portobello Avocado Burger
Roast Large Portobello caps until done, cool to room temperature pat dry and use as a bun for sliced avocado, onion, mustard, tomato, jalapeno and lettuce.

Moroccan Tomatoes
Cut the tops off of 4 tomatoes and save tops.
Hollow tomatoes and fill with a mix of:
Cooked brown rice
1 tsp vegetable bouillon
1 chopped onion
5 chopped dried apricots
Cap the tomatoes with the saved tops.
Bake at 350 for 30 minutes or until done (depends on size of tomato). Serve with quinoa.

Super Soup Supper
Serve any of the lunch soups that you might have leftover on brown rice with a side salad and any non-starchy vegetable for a filling dinner.

Hasselback Zucchini
Place a wooden spoon on either side of a zucchini and slice across the zucchini from end to end.
Bake at 350° for 30 minutes or until golden. Top with Cheezle or Tomato Sauce or both.
Serve hot.

Chili

Into a crock pot mix:

1 can diced carrots	1 tbsp garlic
2 cans kidney beans	1 chopped onion
1 can diced tomatoes	1 cup quinoa
1 can tomato paste	2 tbsp cumin
1 can unsalted corn	1 tbsp paprika
2 cans water	1 chili powder
3 stalks chopped celery	2 tbsp soy sauce
1 chopped green pepper	2 tsp Sriracha

Cook overnight on low. Serve hot.

Quinoa Stuffed Mushrooms

1 tbsp ground chia seeds	8 de-stemmed mushrooms (save stems for filling)
3 Tbsp water	
1 chopped onion	2 tbsp cashews
½ chopped red pepper	1 dash paprika
1 cup cooked quinoa	or Mrs. Dash
2 minced cloves garlic	

Combine chia and water and refrigerate. Meanwhile take a thin slice off the curved top of each mushroom to stabilize and place them onto a parchment-lined baking pan, hollow side up.

In a small amount of vegetable broth, sauté onions and peppers until soft. Add to remaining ingredients (including chia water mix) in food processor and pulse until coarse but not pasty (or chop all ingredients to a fine consistency). Fill mushrooms with quinoa mixture. Bake at 350° for 20-30 minutes or until mushrooms are soft. Time varies with size of mushroom. Dust with paprika or Mrs. Dash. Serve hot.

Taco Salad 2

3/4 cup carrot, peeled and chopped
1/2 cup walnuts
1 tablespoon tomato paste
1/2 cup red onion
1 tsp cumin
1/4-1/2 tsp. chili powder
1-2 cloves minced garlic
Water as needed to blend

Pulse all ingredients to a paste. Serve on a bed of lettuce. Top with Cheezle.

Crabble Cakes

2 ½ cups grated zucchini blotted dry
1 tsp chia seeds powdered in coffee grinder or ground fine with mortar and pestle.
1 avocado halved (reserve other half)
1 cup brown rice
1/4 cup minced onion
1 teaspoon bay seasoning

1 tsp dill relish mixed with other ½ avocado (Avocadill)

Pulse everything but the zucchini and Avocadill. Combine with zucchini and form into flattened balls. Refrigerate on baking dish in refrigerator 1 hour. Remove from refrigerator and place in oven, Bake at 350° for 15-20 minutes or until golden. (Depends on size of crabbles.) Serve hot with a small dollop of Avocadill.

Cauliflower Pizza

1/2 chopped head of cauliflower florets
2 ½ tbsp ground chia seeds
3 tbsp water
1/3 cup almond or oat flour
1/2 tsp oregano
1/2 tsp basil
1/4 tsp garlic powder

Mix chia with water and refrigerate while you chop cauliflower and cook to softness in water.
Squeeze it as dry as you can get it in a clean dish towel.

Stir the flour with the oregano, garlic and basil. (You can make oat flour by processing oats in a blender to flour consistency.) Preheat oven to 450 F.

Place the squeezed-out cauliflower into a medium bowl and add the chia mix. (It should be gloppy.)
Stir in the flour mix.
Form into a ball, and place on a parchment-lined baking sheet. Roll into a circle, 1/4-inch thick between parchment. Bake 25 minutes, or until lightly browned with crispy edges.

Top with Tomato Sauce, chopped onion, mushrooms, peppers, sliced garlic and bake 7 more minutes. Top veggies or sauce with a sprinkle of brewer's yeast or drizzle with Cheezle. Cool a little before slicing for best results.

"Meantballs"

(Meant to make you happy!)

1 lb finely chopped mushrooms
2 shallots chopped
1/2 avocado
1 minced garlic clove
2 cups carrot shredded
1/2 cup chopped parsley
2 cups brown rice
2 tsp chia seeds
3 tbsp water

Mix all ingredients in a bowl and refrigerate 1 hour. Form into balls and bake on parchment-lined sheet for 15-20 minutes or until slightly golden.

Serve with Tomato Sauce, Cheezle or mustard.

You can also form into patty shapes about ½ inch thick to make veggie burgers.

Great crumbled as a meat substitute too.

Enchilada Casserole

1 Eggplant or two zucchini sliced thin lengthwise
1 large onion sliced into disks
1 green or red pepper sliced thin
3 cups salsa or green chili sauce
1 cup quick-cook brown rice
(or already cooked brown rice)
Cheezle

Place eggplant or zucchini onto parchment-lined sheet and bake until soft (+/- 30 minutes) while you cut the vegetables and cook the rice.
Pour 1 cup salsa or sauce on bottom of 9x13 baking pan then layer
 Eggplant/Squash
½ onions and peppers
½ Cheezle
Squash
Rice
1 cup Salsa/Sauce
Squash
½ onions and peppers
½ Cheezle
Squash
1 cup salsa or sauce

Bake 30 minutes or until bubbling. Allow to cool a little before cutting, serve with a sprinkling of brewer's yeast.

90 Money Tips

1. Wrap coins, smooth out crumpled bills and arrange them in the same direction. Learn to respect money.
2. Save all of your change, deposit each Friday, even just $5.00.
3. Look around your house for money, in dressers, jacket pockets, even couches. Deposit what you find.
4. Check to see if you can get a lower rate on phone service. (Prepaid cell phones?)
5. Check competing gas companies to see if you can get a lower rate on heating fuel.
6. Ask your credit card company what you need to do for a lower interest rate or switch to a better card.
7. Move your money to a credit union to take advantage of easier credit.
8. Pay your bills with rewards cards to get points. Shop cards for the best rewards deals.
9. Ask your insurance agent to assess your policy see if you qualify for any new discounts.
10. Consolidate home and car insurance with one company to get lower rates. Compare prices once a year.
11. If you're consolidating bank accounts, keep the one you've had longest to improve your credit.
12. Ask credit card company to set your payment date for when you pay the rest of your bills to avoid late fees.
13. Check statements and receipts every month. Dispute charges you didn't make.
14. Calculate savings on new reduced rate cards, insurance and phone bills. Deposit that much money every month!
15. Attach a grocery list to your refrigerator. Stick to the list when shopping. Take a phone photo of it to the store.
16. Buy store brand foods, the taste is sometimes identical and you can save hundreds a year!
17. Shop for sales items in grocery flyers online before shopping to save time and gas.

18. Shop at grocery stores that offer points on purchases.
19. Buy smart groceries like fruit (chop and freeze it!) and staples early in the month on sale.
20. Make and freeze kid snacks like cookies and cupcakes.
21. Bake two or even three meals at once to save oven electric cost and time later.
22. Separate chips, crackers etc. into snack bags to stretch them and for portion control.
23. Grow a garden. Seeds cost less and you'll get exercise!
24. Go vegetarian once a week, for a month or forever!
25. Refill water bottles with tap water, most brands come from there anyway.
26. Buy generic prescriptions online.
27. Don't buy $1.00 toys. They break, you just buy more!
28. Learn to say no to kids sometimes. (Especially fast food!)
29. Don't buy things for your wardrobe you don't NEED.
30. Don't buy clothes you may be able to wear "someday".
31. Buy clothing and small appliances at thrift stores in good neighborhoods. (It's considered cool now!)
32. Buy gift cards instead of gifts to get points on cards.
33. Ask grandparents for gift cards for older children for Christmas and birthdays, shop sales after.
34. Send gift cards or photos online instead of sending bulky gifts, except to older traditional relatives.
35. Shop after holiday sales for decorations.
36. Slow down to save gas.
37. Check gas prices in your area before you go. (Most prices are available online.)
38. Buy gas away from the highway, it's usually cheaper.
39. Drive only when you have to. Walk or bike if you can.
40. Quit smoking.
41. Don't pay for parking. Take advantage of the exercise!
42. Walk or bike part of the way to work. Most buses have bike racks.
43. Quit the gym and start running or get a subsidy to the Y.
44. Call radio stations for unused promo tickets to concerts.

45. Go fishing as a family activity.
46. Take free lessons online.
47. Go online or use the library for CDs, movies and books.
48. Keep clothing and home items clean and repaired.
49. Borrow tools; return them promptly and in good shape.
50. Get an email account just for coupon memberships.
51. Pack your own lunch.
52. Wash your own car.
53. Trim your own hair. (Only for the skilled!)
54. Co-op babysitting.
55. Go to high school and college productions. (cheap or free!)
56. Use the library for wireless internet, cafes are expensive.
57. Try a pay per month cell phone instead of a two-year contract phone.
58. Completely ignore get rich quick schemes.
59. Take care of your body and teeth with check-ups to avoid more costly visits.
60. Check all doors and windows for repairs and air leaks.
61. Turn off lights in empty rooms, turn down thermostats, close furnace vents and doors in unused rooms.
62. Close windows, add blankets.
63. Take shorter showers.
64. Wash clothes once a week instead of twice, hang towels and curtains to dry.
65. Add a gallon of water to your freezer when it's not full; empty freezers use more electricity.
66. Add a brick to your toilet tank. (Uses less water)
67. Do small repairs like torn weather trim and furnace filters yourself.
68. Use Ebay, Amazon, Craigslist, to sell your unwanted valuables.
69. Use Amazon.com to sell your unused books. Be prompt about sending them!
70. Call ALL your friends and relatives and tell them when you are having a sale.

71. Make flyers for hard to ship sale items and put them on community Facebook pages
72. Sell your designer clothes at a consignment shop.
73. Look for flea markets in your area and if you have enough items, set up a table there.
74. Seek out better opportunities in your current company.
75. Check online job boards regularly for better jobs.
76. Call any well-connected friends and tell them when you are ready for a better job.
77. Join the chamber of commerce to network with professionals for opportunities.
78. Tag and box extra household items for a sale instead of putting them in storage.
79. Make the money you have saved on Fridays work for you by buying cheap new stocks. Research first.
80. Open a mutual fund or bond account. Look for a top producer that matches your lifestyle.
81. Try a self-investing broker like TD Ameritrade and buy stock in companies you believe in.
82. If you are nervous about Wall Street, buy a high interest CD from your bank. Check rates first.
83. Set investment to reinvest dividends. (It adds up!)
84. If you are crafty, set up a booth at a festival. If not set up a flea market booth or have a tag sale.
85. If you can write, start a column or blog or do freelance work. If you can't, do a vlog or podcast.
86. Get a part-time job.
87. Teach guitar, sewing, painting, give makeovers.
88. Ask for a raise.
89. Take the tax deductions!
90. Every month try to stay under budget. Deposit that earned money.

90 Mind Tips

1. Take an IQ test to get a baseline of what you know.
2. Take the test every other month to test progress.
3. Write a list of what you want to learn.
4. Figure out *why* you want to learn.
5. Set a list of priorities. Start with the highest on the list.
6. Set definable short, medium and long-term goals.
7. Check for online classes or videos that can help you.
8. Enlist a friend to accompany you to free classes to keep you going regularly.
9. Search funding, scholarships, and grant websites.
10. Sign up. If you want to take a class, don't wait.
11. Gather supplies from yard sales- microphone, laptop etc.
12. Find a quiet place to study.
13. Set a time for self-directed classes and every day "Go to class".
14. Make a sign and post it on your door or refrigerator to keep family from interrupting your lessons.
15. Get Started. (No procrastinating.)
16. Get Serious. (Take notes refer to them later.)
17. Get Sleep
18. Get Sunshine.
19. Get Someone to help with things you don't understand.
20. Reassess your strategy often. Change what doesn't work.
21. Review but jump ahead if you already know the material to save time
22. Look over your notes before moving on to something new.
23. Write in your journal a list of the main things you are learning.
24. Adjust your situation to fit your learning needs.
25. Pay attention to signs of exhaustion.

26. Keep healthy snacks handy for when you want to get up and "raid the fridge". (Fruit or chopped veggies)
27. Breathe deep cleansing breaths whenever possible.
28. Remember to stretch before sitting down to study to refresh blood-flow to your brain.
29. Find ways to incorporate what you have learned into your day. Ex: Use the foreign language you're learning.
30. While studying listen to soft classical music.
31. If you find you need to use your hands for learning get a stress ball or moldable clay.
32. Take along a book or study guide to waiting rooms.
33. Write interesting facts and observations out longhand in a notebook if you are a tactile learner.
34. Improve your house, body or car with your new skill.
35. Remind yourself NOT to just skim material unless it is in review.
36. Make flash cards for things you find hard to memorize.
37. Write a short essay about your subject.
38. Teach someone a skill you are learning.
39. Calculate with paper whenever possible to reinforce math skills. Sound, motion and sight reinforce learning.
40. Memorize a room; quiz yourself on its contents.
41. Do inner math in the grocery store by adding up prices as you choose items.
42. Meditate at least five minutes a day.
43. Research places to which you want to donate or volunteer to learn more. Don't throw your money away!
44. Many colleges now offer free classes. Test out of the class when you enroll in college to save time and money.
45. Write in a diary during down-time at work.
46. Write carefully by hand whenever you can to improve concentration and your handwriting.
47. Read and compare Orwell's *1984* and Huxley's *Brave New World*.
48. Calculate your salary hours regularly. Are you being paid fairly? Do the math on benefits.

49. Use the margins of your books for notes.
50. Use "mental pegs" to help you remember names and directions.
51. De-clutter your desk or work area regularly.
52. Spend time with intelligent people. We become like the people with whom we spend the most time.
53. Use creative visualization to pre-succeed.
54. Think of interesting ways to barter.
55. Use "drudge work" time to clear your mind.
56. Finish your degree nights, weekends, or online.
57. Don't laugh at racist or sexist jokes.
58. Don't tell racist or sexist jokes.
59. Learn a small instrument like harmonica or ukulele.
60. Use succinct language.
61. Memorize relevant quotations.
62. Embrace your flaws.
63. Believe it can be done. Then do it.
64. Try a new way.
65. Don't jump to conclusions.
66. Get the best information from professionals.
67. Practice affirmations.
68. Don't judge people, instead try to imagine yourself in their shoes.
69. Remind yourself of your higher goals to break bad habits.
70. Take your time making important decisions.
71. Look for your hidden talents in the things you enjoy doing.
72. Recall and relate fond childhood moments to your own children.
73. Delegate responsibilities to teach others and save time.
74. Treat others the way you want to be treated.
75. Take care of your body, it effects your mood and your ability to learn.
76. Use a sunlight bulb in winter.
77. Do crossword puzzles and Sudoku regularly.
78. Write letters to friends and relatives instead of email.

79. Be involved in politics by staying in contact with your representative.
80. Know the easiest route home and to important places and practice describing it.
81. Make things with your hands.
82. Don't talk down to teenagers or children. Learn from them instead, even if it's just tolerance.
83. Collect letters people send you. They may become important later.
84. Exercise to improve your concentration level.
85. Watch dance, opera and theater performances.
86. Keep your eyes for opportunities to learn or to teach. Use them as they present themselves.
87. Keep addresses and phone numbers in your wallet or in your phone.
88. Learn to read music.
89. Try new foods in exotic restaurants.
90. Keep a positive attitude.

90 Body Tips

1. Set a daily calorie goal for food. Stick to it.
2. Set a daily minute goal for exercise. Reach it.
3. Set a daily hygiene routine. Make it habitual.
4. Set a daily grooming routine head to toe.
5. Set a daily hour rest goal.
6. Eat ½ fruit/veg, ¼ protein, ¼ starch daily.
7. Walk, jog or bike instead of driving when possible.
8. Enlist a friend to walk or run with you.
9. Park far away to maximize exercise benefit.
10. Take the stairs instead of the elevator.
11. Drink a glass of cold water as soon as you wake up.
12. Avoid caffeine, sodium and artificial sweeteners.
13. Use moisturizer and body lotion regularly.
14. Do an exfoliating body scrub at least once a month.
15. Brush teeth twice daily.
16. Keep nails clean to avoid viruses.
17. Slough off rough feet skin with pumice.
18. Wash hands before eating and after the bathroom.
19. Lightly condition hair after each shampoo.
20. Deep condition hair once a month.
21. Trim hair every six to eight weeks
22. Wear cotton socks to avoid fungal infections.
23. Do exercises for every muscle group.
24. Alternate upper and lower body exercises daily.
25. Walk or run every day.

26. Take ten deep sustained breaths every hour.
27. Stretch before getting out of bed to energize.
28. Stretch before getting into bed to relax.
29. Get up from your desk and walk every half hour.
30. Take a multivitamin every day.
31. Eat fish once a week or take fish oil tablets.
32. Eat at least one meatless meal a week.
33. Eat fresh fruit and greens every day.
34. Choose fresh produce over frozen.
35. Choose frozen produce over canned.
36. Check expiration dates.
37. Throw away all leftovers every week.
38. Use table salt sparingly if at all.
39. Limit intake of processed food.
40. Limit intake of bleached flours and sugars.
41. Limit intake of alcohol.
42. Drink water before each meal.
43. Quit smoking.
44. Don't use illegal drugs.
45. Limit use of all pain killers.
46. Avoid miracle "anti-aging" potions.
47. Avoid diet pills.
48. Avoid "intelligence" supplements.
49. Eat red meat in moderation if at all.
50. Avoid unnecessary medications.
51. See a doctor for a check-up once a year.
52. See a dentist for a cleaning once a year.

53. Keep yearly prostate/mammogram appointments.
54. Wash wounds and cover immediately.
55. Use douches/colonics only when prescribed.
56. Wash bedclothes in hot water.
57. Use only clean towels.
58. Change toothbrushes every three months.
59. Dress appropriately for the weather.
60. Do facial exercises or chew gum to tighten jaw line.
61. Avoid extreme expressions to prevent wrinkles.
62. Use sunscreen to avoid skin damage.
63. GENTLY remove make-up nightly.
64. Braid long hair to avoid sun and wind damage.
65. Retouch only roots to minimize hair damage.
66. Keep nose and ear hair trimmed. Don't pluck.
67. Don't forget neck hair when shaving.
68. Keep ears clear of dandruff.
69. Sterilize all clippers and nail utensils regularly.
70. Treat sprains with alternating heat and cold.
71. Rest to avoid re-injury.
72. Swim instead of running to strengthen joints.
73. Turn mattress once a month to avoid indentations.
74. Choose a mattress according to your comfort.
75. Close off all light to increase melatonin production.
76. Keep a pre-sleep routine for maximum sleep.
77. Walk instead of standing, run instead of walking.
78. Squeeze a stress ball to lower blood pressure.
79. Hug people you love. Touch is healing.

80. Touch people you know to heal both of you.
81. Don't touch infected skin on anyone even yourself.
82. Cough into your elbow away from people.
83. Blow your nose into a tissue instead of sniffling.
84. Throw out all used tissues immediately.
85. Keep your home dusted to avoid dust mites.
86. Vacuum often to remove allergens.
87. Disinfect bathroom handles regularly.
88. Don't share brushes. (bacteria and bugs)
89. Don't share makeup. (NEVER mascara.)
90. Wash second hand items before wearing.

90 Soul Tips

1. Be grateful for what you have.
2. Be aware of the beauty of your surroundings.
3. Be empathetic at every opportunity.
4. Meditate or pray every day.
5. Simplify your day by cutting out media noise.
6. Look for beauty in all people.
7. Be humble.
8. Notice changes.
9. Notice "Doublespeak".
10. Listen to rival views.
11. Don't force unnecessary changes.
12. Be aware of unsatisfied desires.
13. Lose what you don't need.
14. Listen more than you talk.
15. Stay with your goals. Start over if necessary.
16. Find other ways to get there.
17. Status is worth less than satisfaction.
18. Get educated on world philosophies.
19. Stand up for your beliefs.
20. Do, to teach.
21. Be succinct and direct, but not blunt.
22. Utilize the knowledge of others.
23. Be grateful for flaws.
24. Be focused.
25. Try something new.
26. Ask for advice.
27. Consider the source of advice.
28. Don't always follow advice.
29. Don't always give advice.
30. Recognize your passions. Allow them to help define you.
31. Maintain control of your passions to keep them from harming you.
32. Use your passions to shape your life.
33. Don't let others think for you.
34. Don't think for others.

35. Don't be too sympathetic.
36. Don't play on the sympathy of others.
37. Change with the seasons.
38. Read the news, but not just one source.
39. Don't take the media at face value.
40. Never trust politicians.
41. Vote and write to participate.
42. Be aware of the intentions of others.
43. Ask someone to teach you.
44. Give anonymously.
45. Compliment within earshot.
46. Do something nice for a child.
47. Try harder than you intend to.
48. Don't give up on your dreams.
49. Look for opportunities in failures and disappointment.
50. Set a life goal with your eulogy in mind.
51. Break goals into benchmarks.
52. Enlist help.
53. Never break a chain of kindness.
54. Try something again.
55. Experiment with food.
56. Exercise reason in all things.
57. Be patient.
58. Learn about other cultures.
59. Think it through.
60. Put yourself in someone else's shoes.
61. Advise your best friend, you.
62. Don't blame your parents.
63. Take responsibility for failures.
64. Share credit for success.
65. Control but feel rage and excitement.
66. Be aware of hatred wherever it exists.
67. Explore your own biases.
68. Be merciful.
69. Be honest but kind.
70. Be satisfied with less when you have what you need.

71. Don't always strive to be the alpha.
72. Teach something difficult.
73. Get your hands dirty.
74. Don't worry so much.
75. Don't be apathetic, participate.
76. Give someone a second chance.
77. Be a good citizen.
78. Schedule good deeds.
79. Take the scenic route.
80. Turn off your television.
81. Listen to music.
82. Make music.
83. Appreciate art.
84. Make art.
85. Give to be an example.
86. Keep a tiny treasure of something special.
87. Express kindness.
88. Express appreciation.
89. Accept praise and appreciation.
90. Never stop learning.

Even if you bought the e-book you can scan these and print.

Body Weight Measurements	Neck	Upper Arm	Forearm	Chest/Bust	Waist	Hips	Thigh	Calf
Example 275	16"	17 ½	12	47	47	54	32	18
Week One								
Week Two								
Week Three								
Week Four								
Week Five								
Week Six								
Week Seven								
Week Eight								
Week Nine								
Week Ten								
Week Eleven								
Week Twelve								

Educational goals:

What I've learned:
_____
_____
_____
_____
_____
_____
_____
_____
_____
_____
_____
_____

Monetary Goals:

What I've saved/ new earnings:
_____
_____
_____
_____
_____
_____
_____
_____
_____
_____
_____
_____

Spiritual Goals:

What I've done with my time here:

_____
_____
_____
_____
_____
_____
_____
_____
_____
_____
_____

Body Goals:

What I am able to do with my body now:

_____
_____
_____
_____
_____
_____
_____
_____
_____
_____

www.ingramcontent.com/pod-product-compliance
Lightning Source LLC
Chambersburg PA
CBHW061318040426
42444CB00011B/2700